Nine Discourses for Times of Calamities

Large Print Edition
By
St Alphonsus Liguori
Edited by
Melvin H Waller

St Athanasius Press
All Rights Reserved 2018

ISBN-13: 978-1987625165

ISBN-10: 1987625161

St Athanasius Press
melwaller@gmail.com

Specializing in Reprinting
Catholic Classics

CONTENTS

I. God threatens to chastise us in order to deliver us from chastisement 4

II. Sinners will not believe in the divine threats until chastisement has come upon them 16

III. God is merciful for a season, and then chastises 29

IV. The four principal gates of hell 43

V. External devotions are useless if we do not cleanse our souls from sin 61

VI. God chastises us in this life for our good not for our destruction 73

VII. God chastises us in this life that he may show us mercy in the next 85

VIII. Prayers appease God, and avert from us the chastisement we deserve, provided we purpose to amend 100

IX. Most Holy Mary is the mediatrix of sinners 111

Nine Discourses for Times of Calamities.

FIRST DISCOURSE.

God Threatens to Chastise us in order to deliver us from Chastisement.

"Heu, consolabor super hostibus meis, et vindicabor de inimicis meis."

"Ah, I will comfort Myself over My adversaries: and I will be revenged of My enemies."
— Isa. 1:24.

SUCH is the language of God, when speaking of punishment and vengeance: He says that he is constrained by his justice to take vengeance on his enemies. But, mark you, he begins with the word Heu, "Ah:" this word is an exclamation of grief by which he would give us to understand, that if he were capable of weeping when about to punish, he should weep bitterly at being compelled to afflict us his creatures, whom he has loved so dearly as to give up his life through love for us. "Alas!" says Cornelius à Lapide, "Is uttered by one who is lamenting and not insulting; God signifies by this word that he is grieving, and that he is unwilling to punish sinners." No, this God, who is the Father of mercies, and so much loves us, is not of a disposition to punish and afflict, but rather to pardon and console us. For I know the thoughts that I think towards you, saith the Lord, thoughts of peace, and not of affliction. But someone will say, since such is his character, why does he now punish us? Or, at least, appear as if he meant to punish us? Why so? Because he wishes to be merciful towards us: this anger which he now displays is all mercy and patience.

Let us then, my brethren, understand how the Lord at present appears in wrath, not with a view to our punishment, but in order that we may cleanse ourselves of our sins, and thus enable him to pardon us. Such is the subject of our discourse: GOD THREATENS TO CHASTISE IN ORDER TO DELIVER US FROM CHASTISEMENT.

The threats of men ordinarily proceed from their pride and impotence; whence, if they have it in their power to take vengeance on an object, they threaten nothing, lest they should thereby give their enemies an opportunity of escape. It is only when they want the power to wreak their vengeance that they betake themselves to threats, in order to gratify their passion, by awakening at least the fears of their enemies. Not so the threats of which God makes use; on the contrary, their nature is quite different. His threats do not arise from his inability to chastise, because he can be avenged when he wills; but he bears with us in order to see us penitent, and thus exempt from punishment. Thou hast mercy upon all, because Thou canst do all things, and winkest at the sins of men for the sake of repentance. Neither does he threaten from hatred, in order to torment us with fear; God threatens from love, in order that we may be converted to him, and thereby escape chastisement: he threatens, because he does not wish to see us lost: he threatens, in fine, because he loves our souls. But Thou sparest all, because they are thine, O Lord, who lovest souls. He threatens; but notwithstanding bears with us and delays the infliction, because he wishes to see us converted, not lost. He dealeth patiently for your sake, not willing that any should perish, but that all should return to penance. Thus the threats of God are all acts of tenderness, and amorous calls of his goodness, by which he means to save us from the punishment which we deserve.

Yet forty days, exclaimed Jonas, and Nineve shall

be destroyed. Wretched Ninevites, he cries, the day of your chastisement is come; I announce it to you on the part of God: Know that within forty days Nineve shall be destroyed, and cease to exist. But how comes it that Nineve did penance and was not destroyed? And God saw their works that they were turned from their evil way; and God had mercy. Whereat Jonas was afflicted, and making lamentation before the Lord, said to him: Therefore, I went before Thee into Tarsis, for I knew that Thou art a gracious and merciful God, patient and of much compassion, and easy to forgive evil. He then left Nineve, and was screened from the rays of the burning sun by an ivy which God caused to overshadow his head. But how did the Lord next act? He withered the ivy, whereat Jonas was so much afflicted that he wished for death. God then said to him, Thou hast grieved for the ivy for which Thou hast not labored, nor made it to grow; . . . and shall not I spare Nineve? Thou grievest for the ivy which thou hast not created, and shall not I pardon the men who are the work of my hands?

The destruction which the Lord caused to be held out against Nineve was, according to the explanation of St. Basil, not an actual prophecy, but a simple threat, by which he meant to bring about the conversion of that city. The saint says, that God often appears in wrath because he wishes to deal mercifully with us; and threatens, not with the intention of chastising but of delivering us from chastisement. St. Augustine adds, that when any one cries out to you "Take care," it is a sign he does not mean to injure you. And thus exactly does God act in our regard: he threatens us with chastisement, says St. Jerome, not that he means to inflict it, but to spare us if we profit by the warning. Thou, O Lord, says St. Augustine, art severe, but then most so when Thou wishest to save us; Thou threatenst, but in so threatening Thou hast no other object than to bring us to repentance. The Lord could chastise sinners without warning by a sudden death, which should not leave them time for repentance; but no, he displays his wrath, he brandishes his scourge, in order that he may see them reformed, not punished.

The Lord said to Jeremias: thou shalt say to them—If so be, they will hearken and be converted everyone from his evil way: that I may repent Me of the evil which I think to do unto them. Go, he says, and tell the sinners if they wish to hear you, that if they cease from their sins, I shall spare them the chastisements which I intended to have inflicted on them. And now, my brethren, mark me. The Lord addresses you in a similar way out of my mouth. If you amend, he will revoke the sentence of punishment. St. Jerome says: "God is wroth, not with us, but with our sins;" and St. John Chrysostom adds, that if we remember our sins God will forget them. He desires that we being humbled should reform, and crave pardon of him. Because they arc humbled I will not destroy them.

But, in order to amend, we must be led to it by fear of punishment, otherwise, we never should be brought to change our lives. True it is, God protects him who places hope in his mercy. He is the protector of all who trust in Him. But he who hopes in the mercy of the Lord is always the man who fears his justice. They that fear the Lord have hoped in the Lord: He is their protector and their helper. The Lord often speaks of the rigor of his judgments, and of hell, and of the great number who go thither. Be not afraid of them who kill the body: . . . fear ye Him who, after He hath killed, hath power to cast into hell. Broad is the way that leadeth to destruction, and many there are who enter thereat. And why does the Lord so often speak thus? In order that fear may keep us from vice, and from the passions, and from occasions; and that thus we may reasonably hope for salvation, which is only for the innocent, or the penitent, who hope and fear.

Oh, what strength has not the fear of hell to rein us in from sin, to that end has God created hell. He has created us, and redeemed us by his death, that we might be happy with him; he has imposed upon us the obligation of hoping for eternal life, and on that account encourages us, by saying that all those who hope in him shall be saved. For none of them that wait on Thee shall be confounded. On the other hand, it is his wish and command that we should be in fear of eternal damnation. Some heretics hold, that all who are not in sin should consider themselves as assuredly just and predestined; but these have with reason been condemned by the Council of Trent, because such a presumption is as perilous to salvation as fear is conducive to it. And let Him be your dread, and He shall be a sanctification unto you. The holy fear of God makes man holy. Wherefore David begged of God the grace of fear, in order that fear might destroy in him the inclinations of the flesh. Pierce Thou my flesh with Thy fear.

We should then fear on account of our sins, but

this fear ought not to deject us: it should rather excite us to confidence in the divine mercy, as was the case with the prophet himself. *For Thy name's sake, O Lord, Thou wilt pardon my sin, for it is great.* How is that? Pardon me because my sin is great. Yes, because the divine mercy is most conspicuous in the case of greatest misery; and he who has been the greatest sinner is he who glorifies most the divine mercy, by hoping in God, who has promised to save all those who hope in him. He will save them, because they have hoped in him. For this reason it is, Ecclesiasticus says, that the fear of the Lord bringeth not pain, but joy and gladness: *The fear of the Lord shall delight the heart, and shall give joy and gladness.* Thus this very fear leads to the acquisition of a firm hope in God, which makes the soul happy: *He that feareth the Lord shall tremble at nothing, and shall not be afraid, for He is his hope.* The soul of him that feareth the Lord is blessed. Yes, blessed, because fear draws man away from sin. *The fear of the Lord driveth out sin,* and at the same time infuses into him a great desire of observing the commandments: *Blessed is the man that feareth the Lord: he shall delight exceedingly in His commandments.*

We must, then, persuade ourselves that chastisement is not what the nature of God inclines him to. God, because by his nature he is infinite goodness, says St. Leo, has no other desire than to bless us, and to see us happy. When he punishes, he is obliged to do so in order to satisfy his justice, not to gratify his inclination. Isaias says, that punishment is a work contrary to the heart of God. The Lord shall be angry .... that He may do His work, His strange work; .... His work is strange to Him. And therefore does the Lord say, that he sometimes almost feigns the intention of punishing us. But why does he do so? For this reason: Let every man of you return from his evil way. He does so in order to our reformation, and consequently our exemption from the chastisement deserved by us. The Apostle writes, that God hath mercy on whom He will, and whom He will He hardeneth. With regard to which passage, St. Bernard says, that God of himself wishes to love us, but that we force him to condemn us. He calls himself the Father of mercies, not of vengeance. Whence it comes that his tenderness all springs from himself, and his severity from us.

And who has ever been able to comprehend the greatness of the divine mercies? David says, that God, even while yet angry, feels compassion for us: Thou hast been angry, and hast had mercy on us. "O merciful wrath, which art enkindled but to succor, and threatenest but to pardon," exclaims the abbot Beroncosius. "Thou hast shown," continues David, "Thou hast shown Thy people hard things, Thou hast made us drunk with the wine of sorrow." God discovers himself to us armed with a scourge, but he does so in order to see us penitent and contrite for the offences which we are committing against him: Thou hast given a warning to them that fear Thee: that they may flee before the bow: that Thy beloved may be delivered. He appears with the bow already bent, upon the point of sending off the arrow, but he does not send it off, because he wishes that our terror should bring about amendment, and that thus we should escape the chastisement. That Thy beloved may be delivered. I wish to terrify them, says God, in order that struck by fear they may rise from the bed of sin and return to me. In their affliction they will rise early to Me. Yes, the Lord, although he sees us so ungrateful and worthy of punishment, is eager to free us from it, because how ungrateful so ever we be, he loves us and wishes us well. Give us help from trouble. Thus, in fine, prayed David; and thus ought we to pray. Grant, O Lord, that this scourge which now afflicts us, may open our eyes, so that we de part from sin; because if we do not here have done with it, sin will lead us to eternal damnation, which is a scourge enduring forever.

What shall we then do, my brethren? Do you not see that God is angered? He can no longer bear with us. The Lord is angry. Do you not behold the scourges of God increasing everyday? Our sins increase, says St. John Chrysostom, and our scourges increase likewise. God, my brethren, is wroth: but with all his anger he has commanded me to say, what he formerly commanded to be said by the prophet Zachary: And thou shalt say to them, Thus saith the Lord of Hosts: Turn ye to Me saith the Lord of Hosts, and I will turn to you saith the Lord of Hosts. Sinners, saith the Lord, you have turned your backs upon me, and therefore have constrained me to deprive you of my grace. Do not oblige me to drive you forever from my face, and punish you in hell without hope of pardon. Have done with it: abandon sin, be converted to me, and I promise to pardon you all your offences, and once more to embrace you as my children. Turn ye to Me, saith the Lord of Hosts, and I will turn to you. Why do you wish to perish? (mark how tenderly the Lord speaks.) And why will you die, O house of Israel. Why will you fling yourselves into that burning furnace? Return ye and live. Return to me, I await you with open arms, ready to receive and pardon you.

Doubt not of this, O sinner, continues the Lord. Learn to do well. . . And then come and accuse Me, saith the Lord: if your sins be as scarlet, they shall be made white as snow. Take courage, saith the Lord, change your life, come to me, and if I do not pardon you, accuse me. As if he were to say, Accuse me of lying and bad -faith; but, no, I shall not be unfaithful: your conscience now so black, shall by my grace become as white as snow. No; I will not chastise you if you reform, says the Lord, because I am God, not man. I will not execute the fierceness of My wrath, . . . because I am God, and not man. He says besides, that men never forget an injury, but that when he sees a sinner penitent he forgets all his offences. I will not remember all his iniquities that he hath done. Let us then at once return to God, but let it be at once. We have offended him enough already, let us not tempt his anger, any further. Behold him, he calls us, and is ready to pardon us if we repent of our evil deeds, and promise him to change our lives.

SECOND DISCOURSE.

Sinners will not Believe in the Divine Threats until the Chastisement has come upon Them.

"Si pœnitentiam non egeritis omnes similiter peribitis."

"Except you do penance, you shall all likewise perish."—Luke, 8:5.

AFTER our Lord had commanded our first parents not to eat of the forbidden fruit, unhappy Eve approached the tree and was addressed from it by the serpent, who said to her: Why has God forbidden you to eat of this delightful fruit? Why hath God commanded you? Eve replies: God hath commanded us that we should not eat, and that we should not touch it, lest perhaps we die. Behold the weakness of Eve! The Lord had absolutely threatened them with death, and she now begins to speak of it as doubtful: Lest perhaps we die. If I eat of it, she said, I shall perhaps die. But the devil, seeing that Eve was little in fear of the divine threat, proceeded to encourage her by saying: No, you shall not die the death; and thus he deceived her, and caused her to prevaricate and eat the apple.

Thus, even now, does the enemy continue to deceive so many poor sinners. God threatens: Stop, sinners, and do penance, because if not you shall damn yourselves, as so many others have done: "Except you do penance, you shall all likewise perish." The devil says to them: "No, you shall not die the death." Fear nothing, sin on, continue to enjoy yourselves, because God is merciful; he will pardon you by and by, and you shall be saved. "God," says St. Procopius, "Inspires one with fear, the devil takes it away." God only desires to terrify them by his threats, in order that they may depart from sin, and thus be saved. The devil wishes to destroy that fear, in order that they may persevere in sin, and thus be lost. Many are the wretches who believe the devil in preference to God, and are thus miserably damned. At present, behold the Lord displays his anger and threatens us with chastisement. Who knows how many there may be in this country who have no thought of changing their lives, in the hope that God will be appeased, and that it will be nothing. Hence the subject of the present discourse: SINNERS WILL NOT BELIEVE IN THE DIVINE THREATS, UNTIL THE CHASTISEMENT SHALL HAVE COME UPON THEM. My brethren, if we do not amend, the chastisement will come; if we do not put an end to our crimes, God will.

When Lot was warned by the Lord that he was about to destroy Sodom, Lot at once informed his sons-in-law: Arise, get you out of this place, because the Lord will destroy this city. But they would not believe him: And He seemed to them to speak as it were in jest. They imagined that he wished to sport with their fears, by terrifying them with such a threat. But the punishment overtook them, and they remained to be the sport of the flames. My brethren, what do we expect? God warns us that chastisement hangs over us; let us put a period to our sins, or shall we wait for God to do it? Hear, O sinner, what St. Paul says to you: See, then, the severity and goodness of God—towards them, indeed, that are fallen, the severity; but towards thee the goodness of God, if thou abide in goodness, otherwise thou also shalt be cut off. Consider, says the Apostle, the justice which the Lord has exercised towards so many whom he has punished, and condemned to hell; towards them, indeed, that are fallen, the severity. Consider the mercy with which he has treated you; but towards thee the goodness of God. You must abandon sin; if you change your ways, avoid the occasions of sin, frequent the sacraments, and continue to lead a Christian life, the Lord will remit your punishment, if you abide in goodness; if not, you shall perish, otherwise thou also shalt be cut off. God has already borne with you too long, he can bear with you no longer. God is merciful, but he is just withal; he deals mercifully with those who fear him; he cannot act thus towards the obstinate.

Such a person laments when he sees himself punished, and says, why has God deprived me of my health? Why has he taken from me this child, or this parent? Ah, sinner, what have you said, exclaims Jeremias, your sins have withholden good things from you. It was not the desire of God to deprive you of any blessing, of any gain, of your son, or your parent; it would have been the wish of God to make you happy in all things, but your sins have not allowed him. In the book of Job we read these words: Is it a great matter that God should comfort thee? But thy wicked words hinder this. The Lord would fain console you, but your blasphemy, your murmuring, your obscene words, spoken to the scandal of so many, have prevented him. It is not God, but accursed sin, that renders us miserable and unhappy. Sin maketh nations miserable. We are wrong, says Salvian, in complaining of God when he deals hardly with us. Oh, how much more hardly do we deal with him, repaying with ingratitude the favors which he has bestowed on us!

Sinners imagine that sin procures them happiness; out it is sin which makes them miserable, and afflicted in every respect. *Because thou didst not serve the Lord thy God,* saith the Lord, *in joy and gladness of heart . . . thou shalt serve thy enemy, whom the Lord will send upon thee, in hunger, and thirst, and nakedness, and in want of all things, . . . till He consume thee.* Because thou hast not wished to serve thy God in the peace which all those taste who serve him, thou shalt serve thy enemy in poverty and affliction, until he shall have finished by making thee lose both soul and body. David says that the sinner by his crimes digs himself the pit into which he falls. *He is fallen into the hole he made.* Recollect the prodigal son: he, in order to live without restraint, and banquet as he pleased, left his father; but then, for having left his father, he is reduced to tend swine; reduced to such a degree of misery, that of the vile food with which the swine are filled, he has not wherewithal to fill himself: *And he would fain have filled his belly with the husks the swine did eat, and no man gave unto him.* St. Bernardine of Sienna, relates that a certain impious son dragged his father along the ground. What happened to him afterwards? One day he was himself dragged by his own son in like manner, when, arriving at a certain place, he exclaimed, "No more—stop here, no more—thus far did I drag my own father stop." Baronius mentions a circumstance of a like nature, concerning the daughter of Herodias, who caused John the Baptist to be beheaded. He tells of her, that one day as she was crossing a frozen river, the ice broke under her, and she remained with her head only above the aperture. By dint of her struggles to save herself from death, she had her head severed from her body, and thus died. Oh, how just is not God, when the time of vengeance arrives, he causes the sinner to be caught, and strangled in the net which his own hands have made. The Lord shall be known when He executeth judgments, the sinner hath been caught in the works of his own hands.

Let us tremble, my brethren, when we see others punished, knowing as we do, that we ourselves have deserved the same punishments. When the tower of Siloe fell upon eighteen persons and killed them, the Lord said to many who were present: Think you that they also were debtors above all the men that dwelt in Jerusalem. Do you think that these wretches alone were in debt to God's justice on account of their sins? You are yet debtors to it; and if you do not penance, you shall be punished as well as they: Except you do penance, you shall all likewise perish. O, how many unfortunate men damn themselves by false hope in the divine mercy? Yes, God is merciful, and therefore assists and protects them who hope in his mercy: He is the protector of all that trust in Him. But he assists and protects those only who hope in him, with the intention of changing their lives, not those whose hope is accompanied by a perverse intention of continuing to offend him. The hope of the latter is not acceptable to God, he abominates and punishes it: Their hope the abomination of the soul. Poor sinners, their greatest misery is, that they are lost, and do not know their state. They jest, and they laugh, and they despise the threats of God, as if God had assured them that he should not punish them. "Whence," exclaims St. Bernard, "This accursed security?" Whence, O blind that you are, whence this accursed security, accursed, because it is this security which brings you to hell. I will come to them that are at rest, and dwell securely. The Lord is patient, but when the hour of chastisement arrives, then will he justly condemn to hell those wretches who continue in sin, and live in peace, as if there were no hell for them.

Let sin be no more for us, my brethren; let us be converted if we wish to escape the scourge which hangs over us. If we do not cease from sin, God will be obliged to punish us: For evil-doers shall be cut off. The obstinate are not only finally shut out from Paradise, but hurried off the earth, lest their example should draw others into hell. And let us reflect that these temporal scourges are nothing in comparison with those eternal chastisements, hope of relief from which there is none. Give ear, O sinner, my brother, give ear! For now the axe is laid to the root of the trees. The author of the Imperfect Work, in his comment upon this passage, says: "It is said that the axe is laid, not to the branches, but to the root, so that it will be irreparably exterminated." continues still to live; but when the tree is felled from the root, it then dies, and is cast into the fire. The Lord stands with the scourge in his hand, and you still continue in disgrace with him. The axe is laid to the root. Tremble lest God should make you die in your sins, for if you die thus, you shall be cast into the fire of hell, where your ruin shall be hopeless for eternity.

But, you will say, I have committed many sins

during the past, and the Lord has borne with me. I may, therefore, hope that he will deal mercifully with me for the future. God says, do not speak so: Say not I have sinned, and what harm hath befallen me? For the Most High is a patient rewarder. Do not say so, for God bears with you now, but he will not always bear with you. Pie endures to a certain extent, and then pays off all. Now, therefore, stand up, that I may plead in judgment against you concerning all the kindness of the Lord, said Samuel to the Hebrews. Oh how powerfully does not the abuse of the divine mercies assist in procuring the damnation of the ungrateful! Gather them together as sheep for a sacrifice, and prepare them for the day of slaughter? In the end the herd of those who will not be converted shall be victims of divine justice, and the Lord will condemn them to eternal death, on the day of slaughter, when the day of his vengeance shall have arrived (and we have reason always to be in dread, as long as we are not resolved to abandon sin, lest that day should be already near). God is not mocked; for what things a man shall sow, these, also shall he reap. Sinners expect to mock God by confessing at Easter, or two or three times a year, and then returning to their vomit, and hoping after that to obtain salvation. "He is a mocker, not a penitent," says St.

Isidor, "Who continues to do that for which he is penitent;" but God is not mocked.

What salvation?—What salvation do you expect? For what things a man shall sow, them also shall he reap. What things do you sow? Blasphemy, revenge, theft, impurity: what then do you hope for? He who sows in sin can hope to reap nothing but chastisements and hell. For he that soweth in his flesh, continues the same apostle, of his flesh also shall reap corruption. Continue, impure wretch, continue to live sunk in the mire of your impurity, your impurities will be converted into pitch within your bowels. "A day shall come," says St. Peter Damian, "A day shall come, or rather a night, when your lust shall be turned into pitch to feed an eternal flame within your bowels."

St. John Chrysostom says that some pretend not to see; they see the chastisements, and pretend not to see them. And then others, St. Ambrose says, have no fear of punishment until they see it has overtaken them. 6 To all these it will happen as it did to mankind at the time of the deluge. The patriarch Noah foretold and announced to them the punishments which God had prepared for their sins; but the sinners would not believe him, and notwithstanding that the ark was building before their eyes, they did not change their lives, but went on sinning until the punishment was upon them, until they were smothered in the deluge. And they knew not till the flood came and took them all away. The same happened to the great Babylon, in the Apocalypse, who said: I sit a queen, and I shall not see grief. She persevered in her impurity in the hope of not being punished, but the chastisement at length came as had been predicted! Therefore shall her plagues conic in one day, death and mourning, and famine, and she shall be burnt with fire.

Brother, who knows whether this is not the last call which God may give you? Our Lord says that a certain owner of a vineyard, finding a fig-tree for the third year without fruit, said: Behold, for these three years I come seeking fruit on this fig-tree, and I find none; cut it down therefore, why cumber let it the ground. Then the dresser of the vine replied: Lord, let it alone this year also . . . and if happily it bear fruit—but if not, then, after that, thou shalt cut it down. Let us enter into ourselves, my brethren; for years has God been visiting our souls, and has found no other fruit therein than thorns and thistles, that is to say, sins. Hear how the divine justice ex claims, Cut it down therefore, why cumbereth is the earth? But mercy pleads, Let it alone this year also. Have courage, let us give it one trial more; let us see whether it will not be converted at this other call. But tremblelest the same mercy may not have granted to justice that if you do not now amend, your life shall be cut off, and your soul condemned to hell. Tremble, brother, and take measures that the mouth of the pit do not close over you. Such was the prayer of David: Let not the deep swallow me up; and let not the pit shut her mouth upon me. It is that which sin effects, causing the mouth of the pit, that is, the state of damnation into which, the sinner has fallen, to close over him by degrees. As long as that pit is not entirely closed, there is some hope of escape; but if it once shut, what further hope remains for you? By the closing of the pit, I mean the sinner's being shut out from every glimmer of grace, and stopping at nothing; that being the accomplishment of what the wise man has said: The wicked man, when he is come into the depth of sins, contemneth. He despises the laws of God, admonitions, sermons, excommunications, threats—he despises hell itself; so that persons have been known to say, numbers go to hell, and I amongst the rest. Can the man who speaks so be saved? He can be saved, but it is morally impossible he should. Brother, what do you say? Perhaps you have yourself come to the contempt of the chastisements of God. What do you say? Well, and if you had, what should you do? Should you despair? No; you know what you have to do. Have recourse to the Mother of God. Although you should be in despair, and abandoned by God, Blosius says, that Mary is the hope of the despairing, and the aid of the abandoned. St. Bernard says the same thing when he exclaims, The despairing man who hopes in thee ceases to be desperate. But if God wishes that I should be lost, what hope can there be for me? But, says God, no, my son, I do not wish to see you lost: I desire not the death of the wicked. And what then do you desire, O Lord? I wish him to be converted, and recover the life of my grace: But that the wicked turn from his way and live. Haste then, brother, fling yourself at the feet of Jesus Christ; behold him, see how he stands with his arms open to embrace you, etc. (Here an act of contrition is made.)

THIRD DISCOURSE.

God is Merciful for a Season, and then Chastises.

"Indulsisti genti, Domine, indulsisti genti; numquid glorificatus es?"

"Thou hast been favorable to the nation, O Lord, them hast been favorable to the nation; hast thou been glorified?"
—Isa. 26:15.

LORD, Thou hast often pardoned this people; Thou hast threatened it with destruction by earthquake, by pestilence, in neighboring countries; by the infirmities and death of its own citizens; but Thou hast afterwards taken pity on them: Thou hast been favorable to the nation, O Lord, Thou hast beta favorable to the nation; hast Thou been glorified? Thou hast pardoned us, Thou hast dealt mercifully with us; what hast Thou received in return? Have Thy people abandoned their sins? Have they changed their lives? No, they have gone on from bad to worse; that momentary fear passed, they have begun afresh to offend Thee and provoke Thy wrath.—But, my brethren, perhaps you imagine that God will always wait, always pardon, and never punish? No; GOD IS MERCIFUL FOR A SEASON; THEN HE PUNISHES; this is the subject of this day's discourse.

We must persuade ourselves that God cannot do otherwise than hate sin; he is holiness itself, and therefore cannot but hate that monster, his enemy, whose malice is altogether opposed to the perfection of God. And if God hate sin, he must necessarily hate the sinner who makes league with sin. But to God the wicked and his wickedness are hateful alike. O God, with what an expression of grief and with what reason do you not complain of those who despise you, to take part with your enemy. Hear, O ye heavens, and give ear, O earth, for the Lord hath spoken; I have brought up children, and exalted them; but they have despised Me. Hear, O ye heavens, he says, and give ear, O earth, witness the in gratitude with which I am treated by men. I have brought them up, and exalted them as my children, and they have repaid me with contempt and outrage. The ox knoweth his owner, and the ass his master's crib: but Israel hath not known Me, . . . they are gone away backwards. The beast of the field, the ox and the ass, continues the Lord, know their master, and are grateful to him, but my children have not known me, and have turned their back upon me. But how is this? "Services are remembered even by beasts," says Seneca. The very brutes are grateful to their benefactors; see that dog how he serves and obeys, and is faithful to his master, who feeds him; even the wild beasts, the tiger and the lion are grateful to those who feed them. And God, my brethren, who till now has provided us with everything, who has given us food and raiment: What more? Who has kept us in existence up to the moment when we offended him,—how have we treated him?

How do we purpose to act in future? Do we not perhaps think that there is no punishment, no hell for think to live on as we have been living? Do we not us? But hearken and know that as the Lord cannot but hate sin, because he is holy, so he cannot but chastise it when the sinner is obstinate, because he is just.

When he does chastise, it is not to please himself, but because we drive him to it. The wise man says that God did not create hell, through a desire of condemning man thereto, and that he does not rejoice in their damnation, because he does not wish to see his creatures perish: For God made not death, neither hath He pleasure in the destruction of the living; for He created all things that they might be. No gardener plants a tree in order to cut it down and burn it. It was not God's desire to see us miserable and in torment; and therefore, says St. John Chrysostom, he waits so long before he takes vengeance of the sinner. He waits for our conversion, that he may then be able to use his mercy in our regard. Therefore the Lord waiteth, that He may have mercy on you. Our God, says the same St. John Chrysostom, is in haste to save, and slow to condemn. When there is question of pardon, no sooner has the sinner repented than he is forgiven by God. Scarcely had David said Peccavi, Domino, when he was informed by the prophet that his pardon was already granted: The Lord also hath taken away thy sin. Yes, because "We do not desire pardon so anxiously as he desires to pardon us," says the same holy Doctor. On the other hand, when there is question of punishment, he waits, he admonishes, he sends us warning of it beforehand: For the Lord God doth nothing without revealing His secret to His servants, the prophets.

But when, at length, God sees that we are willing to yield neither to benefits, nor threats, nor admonitions, and that we will not amend, then he is forced by our own selves to punish us, and while punishing us, he will place before our eyes the great mercies he before extended to us: Thou thoughtest unjustly that I shall be like to thee; but I will reprove thee, and set before thy face. He will then say to the sinner, think you, O sinner, that I had forgotten, as you had done, the outrages you put upon me, and the graces I dispensed to you? St. Augustine says that God does not hate but loves us, and that he only hates our sins. He is not wroth with men, says St. Jerome, but with their sins. The saint says, that by his nature God is inclined to benefit us, and that it is we ourselves who oblige him to chastise us, and assume the appearance of severity, which he has not of himself. It is this which David means to express, when he says that the Lord in chastising is like a drunken man who strikes in his sleep: And the Lord was awaked as one out of sleep, and He smote His enemies. Theodoret adds that, as drunkenness is not natural to man, so chastisement does not naturally belong to God; it is we who force him into that wrath which is not his by nature. St. Jerome, reflecting on those words which Jesus Christ on the day of general judgment will address to the reprobate, Depart from Me, you cursed, into everlasting fire, which was prepared for the devil and his angels, inquires, who has prepared this fire for sinners? God perhaps. No, because God never created souls for hell, as the impious Luther taught: this fire has been kindled for sinners by their own sins. He who sows in sin, shall reap chastisement. He that soweth iniquity, shall reap evil. When the soul commits sin, it voluntarily obliges itself to pay the penalty thereof, and thus condemns itself to the pains of hell. For you have said, we have entered into a league with death, and we have made a covenant with hell. Hence St. Ambrose well says, that God has not condemned any one, but that each one is the author of his own chastisement. And the Holy Ghost says, that the sinner shall be consumed by the hatred which he bears himself; with the rod of his anger he shall be consumed. He says Salvian, who offends God has no more cruel enemy than himself, since he himself has caused the torments which he suffers. God, he continues, does not wish to see us in affliction, but it is we who draw down sufferings upon ourselves, and by our sins enkindle the flames in which we are to burn. God punishes us, because we oblige him to punish us.

But I know, you say, the mercies of God are great: no matter how manifold my sins, I have in view a change of life by and by, and God will have mercy upon me. But no, God desires you not to speak thus. And say not the mercy of the Lord is great, He will have mercy on the multitude of my sins. And why has the Lord forbidden you to say so? The reason is this, for mercy and wrath quickly come from Him. Yes, it is true, God has patience, God waits for some sinners; I say some, for there are some whom God does not wait for at all: how many has he not sent to hell immediately after the first transgression? Others he does wait for, but he will not always wait for them; he spares them for a certain time and then punishes. The Lord patiently expecteth, that when the Day of Judgment shall come, He may punish them in the fullness of their sins. Mark well, when the day of judgment shall come: when the day of vengeance shall arrive, in the fullness of their sins. When the measure of sins which God has determined to pardon is filled up, he will punish. Then the Lord will have no mercy, and will chastise unremittingly.

The city of Jericho did not fall during the first circuit made by the Ark, it did not fall at the fifth, or at the sixth, but it fell at last at the seventh. And thus it will happen with thee, says St. Augustine, "At the seventh circuit made by the Ark the city of vanity will fall." God has pardoned you your first sin, your tenth, your seventieth, perhaps your thousandth; he has often called you, now calls you again; tremble lest this should be the last circuit taken by the ark, that is, the last call, after which, if you do not change your life, it will be over with you. For the earth, says the Apostle, that drinketh in the rain which cometh often upon it . . . and bringeth forth thorns and briars is reprobate, and very near unto a curse, whose end is to be burned. That soul, he says, which has often received the waters of divine light and grace, and instead of bearing fruit produces nought but the thorns of sin, is nigh unto a curse, and its end will be to burn eternally in hell fire. In a word, when the period comes, God punishes.

And let us know, that when God wishes to punish, he is able and knows how to do it. The daughter of Sion shall be left . . . as a city that is laid waste. How many cities do we not know to have been destroyed and levelled with the ground, by reason of the sins of the in habitants, whom God could no longer bear with! One day, Jesus Christ being within sight of the city of Jerusalem, gazed upon it, and thinking of the ruin which her crimes were to draw down upon her, our Redeemer, who is so full of compassion for our miseries, began to weep:

Seeing the city, He wept over it, saying: They shall not leave in thee a stone upon a stone, because thou hast not known the time of thy visitation. Poor city, there shall not be left in thee a stone upon a stone, because thou hast not been willing to know the grace which I gave thee in visiting thee with so many benefits, and bestowing upon thee so many tokens of my love; whilst thou hast ungratefully despised me, and driven me away. Jerusalem, Jerusalem, .. how often would I have gathered thy children .. and thou wouldst not, behold your house shall be left to you desolate. Sinful brother, who knows whether God does not at this moment look upon your soul and weep? Perhaps he sees that you will not turn to account this visit which he now pays you, this summons which he gives you to change your life. How often would I . . . and thou wouldst not. How often, says the Lord, have I wished to draw you to me by the lights which I have given you? How often have I called you and you would not hear me? You have been deaf to me and fled from me. Behold your house shall be left to you desolate. Behold I am already on the point of abandoning you, and if I abandon you, your ruin will be inevitable, irreparable.

We would have cured Babylon, but she is not

humbled; let us forsake her. The physician when he sees that the patient will not adopt his remedies, which he himself carries to him with so much kindness, and which the other flings out of the window—what does he do at length? He turns his back upon him and abandons him. My brethren, by how many remedies, by how many inspirations, by how many calls, has not God endeavored to avert damnation from you? What more can he do? If you damn yourself, can you complain of God who has called you in so many different ways? God calls you by the voice of his minister, he calls you by the voice that is within you, he calls you by his favors, he calls you lastly by temporal punishments; in order that you may learn to dread those which are eternal. St. Bernardine of Sienna says that for certain sins, more especially those which are scandalous, there is no more effectual method of doing away with them than by temporal punishments. But when the Lord sees that his favors serve only to make the sinner more insolent in his evil life, when he sees that his threats are disregarded, when he perceives, in a word, that he speaks and is not heard; then he abandons the sinner, and chastises him with eternal death. Therefore does he say, Because I called and you refused . . . and have neglected my reprehensions, I will also laugh in your destruction and will mock when that shall come which you feared. You, says God, have laughed at my words, my threats, and my chastisements, your last chastisement shall come, and then I will laugh at ye. And it (the rod) was turned into a serpent. St. Bruno, in his commentary upon this passage, says, "The rod is turned into a serpent when they will not amend." The eternal will succeed the temporal punishment.

Oh how well does not God know how to chastise, and so to order it that from the instruments and motives of sin should be drawn the chastisement! That they might know that by what things a man sinneth, by the same also he is tormented. The Jews put Jesus Christ to death for fear die Romans should seize on their possessions. If we let Him alone, said they, all will believe in Him, and the Romans will come and take away our place and nation. But the same sin of putting Jesus Christ to death was the cause of their being shortly after despoiled of everything by the Romans. "They feared they should lose temporal possessions," says St. Augustine, "And thought not of eternal life, and so lost both." In trying to save their possessions, they lost their souls; the punishment came, and they lost both. Thus it falls out with many; they lose their souls for the things of earth; but God often condemns them to beggary in this world, and reprobation in the next.

My brethren, provoke no longer the anger of your God, know that in proportion to the multitude of his mercies towards you, in proportion to the length of time he has borne with you, your punishment will be greater if you do not amend. "The Lord makes up for the slowness of his chastisement," says St. Gregory, "By its grievousness when it does come." Woe to thee, Corozain, thus does the Lord speak to a soul that has abused his favors, Woe to thee Bethsaida, for if in Tyre and Sidon had been wrought the mighty things which have been wrought in you, they would have done penance long ago, sitting in sackcloth and ashes. Yes, my brethren, if the graces which have been given to you had been given to a Turk or an Indian, if in Tyre and Sidon had been wrought the mighty works which have been wrought in you, he would have now been a saint, or at least have done great penance for his sins; and have you become a saint? Have you at least done penance for your many mortal sins, for your many evil thoughts, words, and scandals? See you not how God is angry with you? How he stands with his scourge in his hand?

Do you see not death hanging over you.

And what are we to do? You inquire: are we to despair? No, God does not wish us to despair. Let us go with confidence to the throne of grace: that is what we are to do, as St. Paul exhorts us, in order that we may obtain mercy, and find grace in seasonable aid. Let us at once go to the throne of grace that we may receive the pardon of our sins, and the remission of the punishment which overhangs us. By seasonable aid the Apostle means to convey that the aid which God may be willing to lend us today he may deny tomorrow. At once, then, to the throne of grace.

But what is the throne of grace? Jesus Christ, my brethren, is the throne of grace. And He is the propitiation for our sins. Jesus it is who by the merit of his blood can obtain pardon for us, but we must apply immediately. The Redeemer, during his preaching in Juda, cured the sick, and dispensed other favors as he went along; whoever was on the spot to ask a favor of him, obtained it; but whoever was negligent, and allowed him to pass without a request, remained as he was. Who went about doing good. It was this caused St. Augustine to say: "I fear Jesus passing by;" by which he meant to express that when the Lord offers us his grace, we must immediately correspond, doing our utmost to obtain it, that otherwise he will pass on and leave us without it. Today, if you shall hear His voice, harden not your hearts. Today God calls you; give yourself to God today; if you wait for tomorrow, intending to give yourself to him then, perhaps he will have ceased to call, and you will remain deserted.

Mary, the Queen and the mother of mercies, is also a throne of grace, as St. Antoninus says. Hence, if you see that God is angry with you, St. Bonaventure exhorts you to have recourse to the hope of sinners. Go, have recourse to the hope of sinners: Mary is the hope of sinners, Mary who is called the mother of holy hope. But we must take notice that holy hope is the hope of that sinner who repents him of his evil ways, and determines upon a change of life; but if any one pursues an evil course in the hope that Mary will succor and save him, such a hope is false, such a hope is bad and rash. Let us then repent of our sins, resolve to amend, and then have recourse to Mary with a confidence that she will assist and save us. (Act of contrition.)

FOURTH DISCOURSE.

The Four Principal Gates of Hell.

"Defixæ sunt in terra portæ ejus."

"Her gates are sunk into the ground."—Lam. 2:9.

Broad is the way that leadeth to destruction, and many there are who go in thereat. Hell has then different gates, but these gates stand on our earth. Her gates are sunk into the ground. These are the vices by which men offend God, and draw down upon themselves chastisements and eternal death. Amongst the other vices, there are four which send most souls to hell, and on this earth bring upon men the scourges of God; and these four are, HATRED, BLASPHEMY, THEFT, and IMPURITY. Behold, the four gates by which the greater number of souls enter hell; and it is of these four that I mean to speak today, in order that you may amend and cure yourselves of these four vices, otherwise God will cure you of them, but by your own destruction.

1. **HATRED**

The first gate of hell is hatred. As paradise is the kingdom of love, so hell is the kingdom of hatred. Father, says such a person, I am grateful to and love my friends, but I cannot endure him who does me an injury. Now, brother, you must know that the barbarians, the Turks and Indians say and do all this: Do not also the heathens this, says the Lord. To wish well to him who serves you is a natural thing; it is done not only by the infidel, but even by the brutes and wild beasts. But I say to you. Hear what I say to you says Jesus Christ; hear my law, which is a law of love: Love your enemies. I wish, that you, my disciples, should love even your enemies. Do good to them that hate you; you must do good to them that wish you ill, and pray for them that persecute and calumniate you; if you can do nothing else, you must pray for them who persecute you, and then you shall be the children of God your father: that you may be the children of your Father who is in heaven. St. Augustine then is right in saying that it is by love alone a child of God is known from a child of the devil. Thus have the saints always done; they have loved their enemies. A certain woman had traduced the honor of St. Catharine of Sienna, and the saint attended this same woman in her sickness, and ministered to her as a servant. St. Acaius sold his garment to succor one who had taken away his character. St. Ambrose gave to an assassin, who had attempted his life, a daily allowance, in order that he might have wherewithal to live. Such may indeed be called the children of God. Is it a great matter, says St. Thomas of Villanova, that often- when we have received an injury from any one we forgive it at the suit of a friend who pleads for him? And shall we not do the same when God commands it?

Oh, how well grounded a hope of pardon has not he who pardons the man who has offended him. He has the promise of God himself, who says, Forgive, and you shall be forgiven. "By forgiving others," says St. John Chrysostom, "You earn pardon for yourself." But he, on the contrary, who will have vengeance, how can he hope for pardon for his sins? Such a person, in saying the "Our Father," condemns himself when he says: "Forgive us our trespasses, as we forgive them that trespass against us." Then, when such a person wishes to take vengeance, he says to God: Lord, do not pardon me, because I will not pardon my enemies. You give judgment in your own cause, says St. John Chrysostom. But, be assured, that you shall be judged without mercy if you show not mercy to your neighbor. For judgment without mercy to him that hath not done judgment. But how, says St. Augustine, how can he who will not forgive his enemy, according to the command of God, have the face to ask pardon from God for his offences.

If then, my brethren, you wish to have revenge, bid adieu to paradise: Without are dogs. Dogs, on account of their natural fury, are taken to represent the revengeful. These dogs are shut out from paradise; they have a hell in this life; and they shall have hell in the next. "He who is at enmity with any one," says St. John Chrysostom, "Never enjoys peace: he is in everlasting trouble."

But, Father, such a one has taken away my good name, which I will renounce for no one. Such is, for sooth, the proverb, ever in the mouths of those hell hounds who seek for revenge. He has taken away my honor, I must take his life. And is the life of a man at your disposal? God alone is master of life. For it is Thou, O Lord, that hast the power of life and death. Do you wish to take vengeance of your enemy? God wishes to take vengeance of thee. Vengeance belongs to God alone. Revenge is Mine, and I will repay them in due time.

But how else, you say, can my honor be repaired? Well, and in order to repair your honor, you must trample underfoot the honor of God. Do you not know, says St. Paul, that when you transgress the law you dishonor God? Thou by transgression of the law dishonorest God. And what honor is this of yours that you wish to repair? It is the same as the honor of a Turk, of an idolater: a Christian's honor is to obey God, and observe his law.

But other men will look down upon me; and so, for fear you should be looked down upon, you must condemn yourself to hell. But if you forgive, the good will praise you; wherefore it is, that St. John Chrysostom says: If you wish to be revenged, do good to your enemy, because then others will condemn your enemy, and speak well of you. It is not true that he loses his honor, who, when he has been injured or insulted, says: I am a Christian, I neither can nor will be revenged. Such a person gains instead of losing honor, and, besides, saves his soul. On the contrary, he who takes revenge will be punished by God, not only in the other life, but in this also. He is obliged to flee from the justice of men, after having taken that vengeance which will render his life henceforward miserable. What an unhappiness to live a fugitive; to be always in dread of justice; always in dread of the kindred of his victim; tormented with remorse of conscience, and condemned to hell?

And let us further know, my brethren, that revenge and the desire of revenge are alike enormous, are the same sin. Should we at any time receive an offence, what are we to do? When our passion begins to rise, we must have recourse to God, and to the most holy Mary, who will help us, and obtain strength for us to forgive. We should then endeavor to say: Lord, for the love of Thee I forgive the injury that has been done me, and do Thou in Thy mercy forgive me all the injuries I have done Thee.

2. BLASPHEMY.

Let us pass on to the second gate of hell, which is blasphemy. Some, when things go wrong with them, do not attack man, but endeavor to wreak their vengeance upon God himself by blasphemy. Know, my brethren, what manner of sin blasphemy is. A certain author says: "Every sin, compared with blasphemy, is light;" and first of all, St. John Chrysostom says, there is nothing worse than blasphemy. Other sins, says St. Bernard, are committed through frailty, but this only through malice. With reason, then, does St. Bernardine of Sienna call blasphemy a diabolical sin, because the blasphemer, like a demon, attacks God himself. He is worse than those who crucified Jesus Christ, because they did not know him to be God; but he who blasphemes knows him to be God, and insults him face to face. He is worse than the dogs, because dogs do not bite their masters, who feed them, but the blasphemer outrages God, who is at that very moment bestowing favors on him. What punishment, says St. Augustine, will suffice to chastise so horrid a crime? We should not wonder, says Julius III., that the scourges of God do not cease while such a crime exists among us.

Lorino cites the following fact: We read in the preface to the Pragmatic Sanction in France, that King Robert, when praying for the peace of the kingdom, was answered by the crucifix that the kingdom never should have had peace if he had not eradicated blasphemy. The Lord threatens to destroy the kingdom in which this accursed vice reigns. They have blasphemed the Holy One of Israel; . . your land is desolate, . . . if shall be desolate.

Oh, if there were always found someone to do

what St. John Chrysostom; advises: "Strike his mouth, and sanctify thereby thy hand." The mouth of the accursed blasphemer should be struck, and he should then be stoned, as the old law commanded: And he that blasphemeth the name of the Lord, dying let him die: all the multitude shall stone him. Hut it would be better if that were done which St. Louis, King of France, put in force: he commanded by edict that every blasphemer should be branded on the mouth with an iron. A certain nobleman having blasphemed, many persons be sought the king not to inflict that punishment upon him; but St. Louis insisted upon its infliction in every instance; and some taxing him with excessive cruelty on that account, he replied that he would suffer his own mouth to be burned sooner than allow such an outrage to be put upon God in his kingdom.

Tell me, blasphemer, of what country are you? Allow me to tell you, you belong to hell. St. Peter was known in the house of Caiphas for a Galilean by his speech. Surely thou also art one of them, it was said to him, for even thy speech doth discover thee. What is the language of the damned?—blasphemy. And they blasphemed the God of heaven because of their pains and wounds. What do you gain, my brethren, by these your blasphemies, you gain no honor by them. Blasphemers are abhorred even by their blasphemous companions. Do you gain any temporal advantage. Do you not see that this accursed vice keeps us forever in beggary? Sin maketh nations miserable. Do you derive pleasure from it? What pleasure do you derive from blaspheming God? The pleasure of the damned; and that moment of madness past, what pain and bitterness does it not leave in your heart? Resolve to rid yourself of this vice in any event. Take care, if you do not abandon it now, that you will not carry it with you to death, as has happened to so many who have died with blasphemy in their mouths. But, Father, what can I do when the madness comes upon me? Good God, and are there no other means of working it off than by blasphemy? Say, cursed be my sins. Mother of God, assist me, give me patience; your passion, your anger, will pass off quickly, and you will find yourself in the grace of God after the trial. If you do not act thus, you will find yourself more afflicted and more lost than before.

3. THEFT.

Let us now pass on to the consideration of the third great gate of hell by which so large a portion of the damned enter; I mean theft. Some, so to speak, adore money as their God, and look upon it as the object of all their desires. The idols of the Gentiles are silver and gold. But the sentence of condemnation has already been pronounced against such: Nor thieves . . . nor extortioners shall possess the kingdom of God. It is true that theft is not the most enormous of sins, but St. Antoninus says that it very much endangers salvation. The reason is because for the remission of other sins true repentance only is required; but repentance is not enough for the remission of theft: there must be restitution, and this is made with difficulty. A certain hermit had once the following vision: he saw Lucifer seated on a throne, and inquiring of one of his demons why he had been so long about returning. The latter replied that he had been detained by his endeavors to tempt a thief not to restore what he had stolen. Let this fool be severely punished, said Lucifer. To what purpose have you spent this time? Do you not know that he who has taken the property of another never restores it? And, in truth, so it is: the property of another becomes to him who takes it like his own blood; and the pain of suffering one's blood to be drawn for another is very difficult to endure. We learn it every day from experience: innumerable thefts take place; how much restitution do you see?

My brethren, see that you take not the property of your neighbor, and if during the past you have ever failed in this respect, make restitution as soon as possible. If you cannot at once make full restitution, do it by degrees. Know that the property of another in your possession will not only be the means of bringing you to hell, but will make you miserable even in this life. Thou hast despoiled others, says the prophet, and others shall despoil thee. Because thou hast spoiled many nations, all that shall be left of the people shall spoil thee. The property of another brings with it a curse which will fall upon the entire house of the thief. This is the curse that goeth forth over the face of the earth, . . . and it shall come to the house of the thief; that is to say (as St. Gregory Nazianzen explains it), that the thief shall lose not only the stolen property, but his own The goods of another are as fire and smoke to consume everything that comes in their way.

Remember well, mothers and wives, when children or husbands bring home the property of their neighbor, remember well to chide and reprove them; not to applaud their action, or even consent to it by silence. Tobias hearing a lamb bleat in his house, Take heed, said he, lest perhaps it be stolen; restore ye it to its owners. St. Augustine says that Tobias, because he loved God, did not wish to hear the sound of theft in his house. Some persons take the property of their neighbor, and then are fain to quiet their consciences by alms-deeds. Christ, says St. John Chrysostom, will not be fed with the plunder of others. The sins of this kind, committed by the great, are acts of injustice, the injuries that they inflict upon others, the taking from the poor of what is their due. These are descriptions of theft which require perfect restitution, and a restitution most difficult of all to make, and most likely to be the cause of one's damnation.

4. IMPURITY.

We have now, lastly, to speak of the fourth gate of hell, which is impurity, and it is by this gate that the greater number of the damned enter. Some will say that it is a trifling sin. Is it a trifling sin? It is a mortal sin. St. Antoninus writes, that such is the nauseousness of this sin; that the devils themselves cannot endure it. Moreover, the Doctors of the Church say that certain demons, who have been superior to the rest, remembering their ancient dignity, disdain tempting to so loathsome a sin. Consider then how disgusting he must be to God, who, like a dog, is ever returning to his vomit, or wallowing like a pig in the stinking mire of this accursed vice. *The dog is returned to his vomit; and the sow that was washed, to her rolling in the mire.*

The impure say, moreover, God has compassion on us who are subject to this vice, because he knows that we are flesh. What do you say? God has compassion on this vice. But you must know that the most horrible chastisements with which God has ever visited the earth have been drawn down by this vice. St. Jerome says that this is the only sin of which we read that it caused God to repent him of having made man. *It repented Him that had made man;. . . for all flesh had corrupted its way.* Wherefore it is, St. Jerome says, that there is no sin which God punishes so rigorously, even upon earth, as this. He once sent fire from heaven upon five cities, and consumed all their inhabitants for this sin. Principally on account of this sin did God destroy mankind, with the exception of eight persons, by the deluge. It is a sin which God punishes, not only in the other life, but in this also. In confirmation of this, you have only to enter the hospitals, and see there the many poor young men, who were once strong and robust, but are now weak, squalid, full of pains, tormented with lancets and caustic, and ulcers, all through this accursed vice. Because thou hast forgotten Me and cast Me off behind My back, bear thou also thy wickedness and thy fornications. Because, says God, you have forgotten me and turned your back upon me, for a miserable pleasure of the flesh, I am resolved that even in this life you shall pay the forfeit of your wickedness.

You say, God has compassion upon men subject this sin. But it is this sin that sends most men to hell St Remigius says, that the greater number of the damned are in hell through this vice. Father Segneri writes, that as this vice fills the world with sinners, so it fills hell with damned souls; and before him St. Bernardine of Sienna wrote: "This sin draws the whole world, as it were, into sin." And before him St. Bernard, St. Isidore, said, that "The human race is brought under the power of the devil more by lust than by all the other vices." The reason is, because this vice proceeds from the natural inclination of the flesh. Hence the angelic Doctor says, that the devil does not take such complacency in securing the commission of any other sin as of this, because the person who is plunged in this infernal mire remains fast therein, and almost wholly unable to free himself more. "No one is so obstinate in sin as the impure," says St. Thomas of Villanova. Moreover, this vice deprives one of all light, for the impure man becomes so blind as almost wholly to forget God, says St. Laurence Justinian; which is in accordance with what is said by the prophet Osee: They will not set their thoughts to return to their God; for the spirit of fornication is in the midst of them, and they have not known God. The impure man knows not God; he obeys neither God nor reason, as St. Jerome says; he obeys only the sensual appetite which causes him to act the beast.

This sin, because it flatters, makes us fall at once into the habit of it, a habit which some carry with them even to death. You see husbands, and decrepit old men, indulge in the same thoughts and committing the same sins that they committed in their youth. And because sins of this kind are so easily committed, they become multiplied without number. Ask of the sinner how many impure thoughts he has consented to: he will tell you he cannot remember. But, brother, if you cannot tell the number, God can; and you know that a single immodest thought is enough to send you to hell.

How many immodest words have you spoken, in which you took delight yourself, and by which you scandalized your neighbor? From thoughts and words you proceed to acts, and to those innumerable impurities which those wretches roll and wallow in like swine, without ever being satisfied, for this vice is never satisfied.

But, Father, you will say, how can I hold out against the innumerable temptations which assail me? I am weak, I am flesh. And since you are weak, why not recommend yourself to God, and to most holy Mary, who is the mother of purity? Since you are flesh, why do you throw yourself in the way of sin? Why do you not mortify your eyes? Why do you gaze upon those objects whence temptations flow? St. Aloysius never raised his eyes to look even upon his mother.

It is to be remarked, moreover, that this sin brings with it innumerable others: enmities, thefts, and, more especially, sacrilegious confessions and Communions, by reason of the shame which will not allow these impurities to be disclosed in confession. And let us remark here in passing, that it is sacrilege above all things, that brings upon us sickness and death; for, says the Apostle, He that eateth and drinketh unworthily, eateth and drinketh judgment to himself, not discerning the body of the Lord; and then he adds: therefore are many infirm and weak among you. And St. John Chrysostom, in explanation of that passage, says that St. Paul speaks of persons who were chastised with bodily infirmities, because they received the sacrament with a guilty conscience.

My brethren, should you ever have been sunk in this vice, I do not bid you be disheartened, but arise at once from this foul and infernal pit; beg of God forthwith to give you light, and stretch out his hand to you. The first thing that you have to do is to break with the occasion of sin: without that, preaching and tears and resolutions and confessions, all are lost. Remove the occasions, and then constantly recommend yourself to God, and to Mary the mother of purity. No matter how grievously you may be tempted, do not be discouraged by the temptation; at once call to your aid Jesus and Mary, pronouncing their sacred names. These blessed names have the virtue of making the devil fly, and stifling that hellish flame within you. If the devil persist in tempting you, persevere in calling upon Jesus and Mary, and certainly you shall not fall. In order to rid yourself of your evil habits, undertake some special devotion to our Lady; begin to fast in her honor upon Saturdays; contrive to visit her image every day, and beg of her to obtain for you deliverance from that vice. Every morning immediately after rising, never omit saying three "Hail Marys" in honor of her purity and do the same when going to bed; and above all things, as I have said, when the temptation is most troublesome, call quickly upon Jesus and Mary. Beware, brother, if you do not be converted now, you may never be converted. (Act of contrition.)

FIFTH DISCOURSE.

External Devotions are Useless if we do not Cleanse our Souls from Sin.

"Et nunc nolite illudere ut forte constringantur vincula tua."

"And now do not mock, lest your bonds be tied strait." —Isa. 27:22.

GOD commands Jonas to go and preach to Ninive. Jonas, instead of obeying God, flies by sea towards Tharsis. But, behold, a great tempest threatens to sink the ship; and Jonas knowing that the tempest was raised in punishment of his disobedience, said to the crew of the vessel: Take me up and cast me into the sea, and the sea shall be calm to you; for I know that for my sake this great tempest is upon you. And they actually did cast him into the sea, and the tempest ceased there upon. And the sea ceased from raging. Then if Jonas had not been thrown into the sea the tempest should not have ceased. Consider well, my brethren, what we are to learn from this. It is, that if we do not cast sin out of our souls, the tempest, that is, the scourge of God, will not cease. The tempest is excited by our sins; the tempest which is hurrying us to destruction. Our iniquities, like the wind, hare taken us away. Behold, we have penitential exercises, novenas, and exposition of the Blessed Sacrament; but to what purpose are those if we be not converted, if we do not rid our souls of sin? The subject of our discourse is: EXTERNAL DEVOTIONS ARE USELESS, IF WE DO NOT ABANDON OUR SINS; because otherwise we cannot please God.

It is said that the pain is not removed before the thorn has been plucked out. St. Jerome writes that God is never angered, since anger is passion, and passion is incompatible with God. He is always tranquil; and even in the act of punishing, his tranquility is not in the least disturbed. But Thou being master of power, judgest with tranquility. But the malice of mortal sin is so great, that if God were capable of wrath and affliction, it would enrage and afflict him. It is this that sinners do as far as in them lies, according to that of Isaias: But they provoked to wrath, and afflicted the spirit of His Holy one. Moses writes, that when God was about to send the deluge, he declared himself to be so much afflicted by the sins of men as to be obliged to exterminate them from the earth. And being touched inwardly with sorrow of heart, He said, I will destroy man whom I have created, from the face of the earth.

St. John Chrysostom says that sin is the only cause of all our sufferings and chastisements. Commenting upon these words in Genesis which the Lord spoke after the deluge, I will place My bow in the clouds, St. Ambrose remarks that God does not say I will place my arrow, but my bow, in the clouds; giving us thereby to understand that it is always the sinner who fixes the arrow in the bow of God by provoking him to chastisement.

If we wish to be pleasing to the Lord, we must remove the cause of his anger, which is sin. The man sick of the palsy besought Jesus Christ to restore the health of his body; but, before granting his request, our Lord first restored his soul's health by giving him sorrow for his sins, and then saying to him: Be of good heart, son; thy sins are forgiven thee. St. Thomas says that the Redeemer first removed the cause of his infirmity, namely, his sins, and then freed him from the infirmity itself. "He asked for the health of the body, and the Lord gave him the health of the soul; because, like a good physician, he wished to take away the root of the evil." Sin is the root of every evil, as we find in St.

Bernardine of Sienna. Hence the Lord after having healed him, warned him against sin in these words. Go thy way, and sin no more, lest something worse befall thee. Ecclesiasticus said the same before our Lord: My son, in thy sickness . . . cleanse thy heart from sin, . . . and then give place to the physician. You must first apply to the physician of the soul in order that he may free you from your sins, and then to the physician of the body that he may cure you of your disease.

In a word, the cause of all our chastisements is sin; and still more than sin, our obstinacy in it, as St. Basil says. We have offended God, and are, notwithstanding, unwilling to do penance. When God calls by the voice of his punishment, he desires that he should be heard; if he be not, he shall be compelled by ourselves to curse us: But if thou wilt not hear the voice of the Lord thy God . . . all these curses shall come upon thee; . . . cursed shalt thou be in the city, cursed in the field. . . . When we offend God, we provoke all creatures to punish us. St. Anselm says that in the same manner as a servant, when he offends his master, draws down upon him the wrath, not only of his master, but of the whole family; so we, when we offend God, excite against us the anger of all creatures. And

St. Gregory says that we have more especially irritated against us those creatures which we have made use of against our Creator. God's mercy holds in those creatures that they may not afflict us, but when he sees that we make no account of his threats, and continue to live on in our former way, he will then make use of those creatures to take vengeance on us for the injuries we have done him: He will arm the creature for the revenge of His enemies. And the whole world shall fight with Him against the unwise. "There is no creature," says St. John Chrysostom, "Which will not feel anger when it sees its Lord in anger."

If then, my brethren, we do not appease God by our conversion, we never shall be free from chastisement. What folly, says St. Gregory, could be more extreme than to imagine that God should cease to chastise before we should have ceased to offend? Many now come to the church, and hear the sermon, but go away without confession, or change of life. If we do not remove the cause of the scourge, how can we expect to be delivered from the scourge itself. Such is the reflection of St. Jerome. We continue to irritate God, and then wonder that God should continue to chastise us. "Impure as we are," says Salvian, "We wonder why we should be so miserable." Do we think that God is appeased by the mere circumstance of our appearing at church without repenting of our sins, without restoring the property or character of our neighbor, without avoiding those occasions of sin which keep us at a distance from God? Ah, let us not mock the Lord! And now do not mock, lest your bonds be tied strait. Do not mock God, says the prophet, lest those bonds which are securing you for hell be tied strait. Cornelius à Lapide, in commenting on the above passage of Isaias, says that when the fox is caught in the snare, its efforts to disengage itself only serve to entangle it the more. "So also will it happen to sinners who, while mocking at God's threats and punishments, become more and more involved in them." My brethren, let us have done; let us no more irritate God, the chastisement is near at hand: *For I have heard of the Lord the God of Hosts*, continues the prophet, *a consumption, and a cutting short upon all the earth*. I am not the prophet Isaias, but I can say that, see the scourge which is hanging over us if we do not be converted.

Hear how the Lord says to you: *Who requires these things at your hands?* Who required your perpetual exercises and your visits of devotion to the church? I will have nothing from you unless you abandon sin: Offer sacrifice no more in vain. Of what use are your devotions if you do not amend your lives. My soul hateth . . . your solemnities. Know, says the Lord, that your homage and external devotions are hateful to my soul whilst you think by these to avert your chastisement without removing your offences: With burnt offerings Thou wilt not be delighted; a sacrifice to God is an afflicted spirit. No devotions, or alms, or penitential works are accepted by God from a soul in the state of sin, and without repentance. God accepts the acts of him alone who is contrite for his sin, and resolved upon a change of life.

Oh, surely God is not to be mocked! I never commanded you, he says, to perform those devotions and acts of penance: For I spoke not to your fathers . . . concerning the matter of burnt offering and sacrifices, but this thing I commanded them, saying: Hearken to My voice, and I will be your God. What I wish of you, says God, is, that you hear my voice and change your life, and make a good confession, with real sorrow, for you must know yourselves, that your other confessions, followed by so many relapses, have been worth nothing. I wish that you should do violence to yourselves in breaking with that connection, with that company. I wish that you should endeavor to restore that property, to make good to your neighbor such a loss. Hearken to My voice, obey My command, and I will be your God. I will then be to you the God of mercy, such as you would have me to be. Cardinal Hugo, in his comment upon these words of our Lord, in the Gospel according to St. Matthew: He that hath ears to hear, let him hear, says: "Some have ears, but ears which do not serve them for hearing." How many attend sermons and receive admonitions from the confessor, in which they are told all that they must do in order to please God; but they leave the church only to live worse than before. How can God be appeased by such, or how can such be delivered from the divine chastisement? Offer up the sacrifice of justice, and trust in the Lord, says David. Honor God not in appearance, but by works. It is that which is meant by "The sacrifice of justice;" honor him by bewailing your sins, by the frequentation of the sacraments, by a change of life and then hope in the Lord; but to hope while you continue the state of sin, is not hope—it is rashness, it is a deceit of the enemy, and renders you more odious in the sight of God, and more deserving of punishment.

My brethren, you see that the Lord is in wrath, that he already has his hand lifted to strike with the scourge which threatens us; how do you think to escape? Who hath showed you to flee from the wrath to come? Bring forth, therefore, fruit worthy of penance, says St. John the Baptist, preaching to the Jews of his day. You must do penance, but penance deserving of his pardon; that is, it must be true and resolute. Your anger must he changed into meekness, by the forgiveness of those who offend you; your intemperance must become abstinence, by observing the fasts commanded, at least, by the Church; and by abstaining from the immoderate use of intoxicating drinks, which change man into a beast: therefore you must avoid the public house; impurity must give way in you to chastity, by not returning to that filthy vomit, by resisting evil thoughts, by not using bad words, by fleeing from bad companions and dangerous conversation. You must bring forth fruit worthy of penance, and the bringing forth of such fruit implies also that we attend to the service of God, and endeavor to serve him more than we offended him; For, as you have yielded your members to serve uncleanness and iniquity, . . . so now yield your members to love justice. Thus have done a St. Mary Magdalen, a St. Augustine, a St. Mary of Egypt, a St. Margaret of

Cortona, who by their works of penance and sanctification rendered themselves more dear to God than others who had been less sinful, but more tepid. St. Gregory says: "For the most part, a fervent life after sin is the more pleasing to God than a life which, though innocent, is tepid." And thus does the saint explain the following passage of the Gospel: There shall be joy in heaven upon one sinner that doth penance, more than upon ninety-nine just who need not penance. This is understood of the sinner who, after having arisen from sin, sets about serving God with more fervor than others who have long been just.

This is to bring forth fruit worthy of penance, not content one's self with hearing sermons and visiting the church, without abandoning sin, or avoiding the occasion of it. To act thus, is rather a mockery of God, and calculated to excite him to greater wrath. And, think not, pursues St. John the Baptist, think not to say within yourselves, We have Abraham for our father. It will not do to say, we have the Mother of God to assist us, we have our patron saint to procure us deliverance; because if we do not abandon our sins the saints cannot help us. The saints are the friends of God; hence they not only have no inclination, but they would even feel ashamed, to succor the obstinate. Let us tremble, because the Lord has already published the sentence: Every tree that bringeth not forth good fruit, shall be cut down and cast into the fire. Brother, how many years have you been in the world? Tell me what fruit of good works have you hitherto borne, what honor have you rendered to God by your life? Sin, outrage, con tempt, such are the fruit you have borne, the honor you have rendered to God.—God now in his mercy gives you time for penance, in order that you may bewail the injuries you have done him, and love him the remainder of your days. What do you intend to do? What have you resolved upon? Resolve at once to give yourself to God. What do you expect, unless that if you do not at once turn to God, you shall be cut down and cast into the fire of hell.

But let us now bring our instruction to a conclusion; the Lord has sent me to preach here today, and has inspired you to come and listen to me, because he wishes to spare you the punishment which threatens you, if you do really turn to him: Leave not out one word, if so be they will hearken and be converted, everyone from his evil way, that I may repent me of the evil which I think to do unto them. The Lord has desired me to tell you on his part that he is willing to relent, and withdraw the scourge which he meant to inflict upon you: That I may repent me of the evil which I think to do unto them; but on this condition, if so be they will hearken and be converted everyone from his evil way, if they truly reform, otherwise he will put his threat in execution.—Tremble then if you be not yet resolved to change your life.

But, on the other hand, be joyful if you mean to turn in good earnest to God. Let the heart of them rejoice that seek the Lord, because God is all tenderness and love to those that seek him. The Lord is good . . . to the soul that seeketh Him. Neither does the Lord know how to reject a heart humble and contrite for its offences. A contrite and humble heart, O God, Thou wilt not despise. Let us be joyful, then, if we have the good intention of changing our lives, and if, on seeing ourselves guilty of so many sins before the Lord, we stand very much in fear of the divine judgments, let us have recourse to the Mother of mercies, the most holy Mary, who defends and secures from the divine vengeance all those who take refuge under her mantle.—"I am the citadel of all those who fly to me;" thus is she made to speak by St. John Damascene. (Act of contrition.)

SIXTH DISCOURSE.

God Chastises us in this Life for our Good, not for our Destruction.

"Non enim delectaris in perditionibus nostris."

"For thou art not delighted in our being lost."
—Job, 3:22.

LET us feel persuaded, my brethren, that there is no one who loves us more than God. St. Teresa says that God loves us more than we love ourselves. He has loved us from eternity. Yea, I have loved thee with an everlasting love. It is the love he has borne us which has drawn us from nothing-, and given us being. Therefore have I drawn Thee, taking pity on Thee. Hence, when God chastises us upon the earth, it is not because he wishes to injure us, but because he wishes us well, and loves us. But of this every one is sure that worshippeth Thee, that his life, if it be under trial, shall be crowned: and if it be under tribulation, shall be delivered. So spoke Sara the wife of Tobias: Lord, he who serves thee is sure that after the trial shall have passed he shall be crowned, and that after tribulation he shall be spared the punishment which he deserved: For Thou art not delighted in our being lost: because after a storm Thou makest a calm, and after tears and weeping Thou pourest in joyfulness. After the tempest of chastisement he gives us peace, and after mourning, joy and gladness.

My brethren, let us convince ourselves of what I have undertaken to show you today, namely, that God does not afflict us in this life for our injury but for our good, in order that we may cease from sin, and by recovering his grace escape eternal punishment.

And I will give My fear in their heart, that they may not revolt from Me. The Lord says that he infuses his fear into our hearts, in order that he may enable us to triumph over our passion for earthly pleasures, for which, ungrateful that we are, we have left him. And when sinners have left him, how does he make them look into themselves, and recover his grace? By putting on the appearance of anger, and chastising them in this life: In Thy anger Thou shalt break the people in pieces. Another version, according to St. Augustine, has: "In thy wrath thou shalt conduct the people." The saint inquiring, What is the meaning of his conducting the people in his wrath, he then replies: "Thou, O Lord, fillest us with tribulations, in order that, being thus afflicted, we may abandon our sins and return to Thee."

When the mother wishes to wean her infant how does she proceed? She puts gall upon her breast. Thus the Lord endeavors to draw our souls to himself, and wean them from the pleasures of this earth, which make them live in forgetfulness of their eternal salvation; he fills with bitterness all their pleasures, pomps, and possessions, in order that, not finding peace in those things, they may turn to God, who alone can satisfy them. In their affliction they will rise early to Me. God says within himself, If I allow those sinners to enjoy their pleasures undisturbed, they will remain in the sleep of sin: they must be afflicted, in order that, recovering from their lethargy, they may return to me. When they shall be in tribulation they will say: Come, let us return to the Lord, for He hath taken us, and He will heal us; He will strike and He will cure us. What shall become of us, say those sinners, as they enter into themselves, if we do not turn from our evil courses? God will not be appeased, and will with justice continue to punish us: come on, let us retrace our steps; for he will cure us, and if he has afflicted us just now, he will upon our return think of consoling us with his mercy.

In the day of my trouble I sought God, . . . and I was not deceived because he raised me up. For this reason does the prophet thank the Lord that he hath humbled him after his sin; because he was thus taught to observe the divine laws: It is good for me that Thou hast humbled me, that I may learn Thy justifications. Tribulation is for the sinner at once a punishment and a grace, says St. Augustine. It is a punishment inasmuch as it has been drawn down upon him by his sins; but it is a grace, and an important grace, inasmuch as it may ward eternal destruction from him, and is an assurance that God means to deal mercifully with him if he look into himself, and receive with thankfulness that tribulation which has opened his eyes to his miserable condition, and invites him to return to God. Let us then be converted, my brethren, and we shall escape from our several chastisements: "Why should he who accepts chastisement as a grace be afraid after receiving it?" says St. Augustine. He who turns to God, smarting from the scourge, has no longer anything to fear, because God scourges only in order that we may return to him; and this end once obtained, the Lord will scourge us no more.

St. Bernard says that it is impossible to pass from the pleasures of the earth to those of Paradise: "It is difficult, even impossible, for anyone to enjoy present and future goods, to pass from delights to delights." Therefore does the Lord say, Envy not the man who prospereth in his way, the man who doth unjust things. "Does he prosper?" says St. Augustine; "Ay, but 'in his own way.' And do you suffer? You do, but it is in the way of God." You who walk before God are in tribulation, but he, evil as is his way, prospers. Mark now what the saint says in conclusion: "He has prosperity in this life, he shall be miserable in the next; you have tribulation in this life, you shall be happy in the next." Be glad, therefore, O sinners, and thank God when he punishes you in this life, and takes vengeance of your sins; because you may know thereby that he means to treat you with mercy in the next. Thou wast a merciful God to them, and taking vengeance on their inventions. The Lord when he chastises us has not chastisement so much in view as our conversion. God said to Nabuchodonozor: Thou shalt eat grass like an ox, and seven times shall pass over thee, till then know that the Most High ruleth in the kingdom of men. For seven years, Nabuchodonozor, shalt thou be compelled to feed upon grass like a beast in order that thou mayest know I am the Lord; that it is I who give kingdoms, and take them away; and that thou mayest thus be cured of thy pride. And in fact this judgment did cause the haughty king to enter into himself and change; so that, after having been restored to his former condition, he said: Therefore I, Nabuchodonozor, do now praise and magnify the King of heaven: And God gave him back his kingdom. "He willingly changed his sentence," says St. Jerome, "Because he saw his works changed."

Unhappy we, says the same saint, when God does not punish us in this life! It is a sign that he means us for eternal chastisements. What do we conclude, he continues, when the surgeon sees the flesh about to mortify, and does not cut it away, we conclude that he abandons the patient to death? God spares the sinner in this life, says St. Gregory, only to chastise him in the next. Woe to those sinners to whom God has ceased to speak, and appears not to be in anger. I will cease and be angry no more. The Lord then goes on to say: But thou hast provoked Me in all these things: . . . and thou shalt know that I am the Lord, . . . that thou mayest remember, and be confounded. A day will come, he says, ungrateful sinner, when you shall know what I am; then shall you remember the graces I have given you, and see with confusion your black ingratitude.

Woe to the sinner who goes on in his evil life, and whom God in his vengeance suffers to accomplish his perverse desires, according to what is said by the prophet: Israel hearkened not to Me, so I let them go according to the desires of their heart. It is a sign that the Lord wishes to reward them on this earth for whatever little good they may have done, and reserves the chastisement of their sins for eternity. Speaking of the sinner whom he treats thus in this life, the Lord says: Let us have pity on the wicked, but he will not learn justice, . . . and he shall not see the glory of the Lord. Thus does the poor sinner hasten on to his ruin, because seeing himself prosperous, he deceives himself into the expectation that as God is dealing mercifully with him now, he will continue to do the same; and by this delusion he will be led to live on in his sins. But will the Lord be always thus merciful to him? No, the day of punishment will come at length, when he shall be excluded from paradise, and flung into the dungeon of the rebels: And he shall not see the glory of the Lord. "Let us have pity on the wicked; far from me be this mercy," says St. Jerome. Lord, he says, extend not to me this dreadful pity; if I have offended Thee, let me be chastised for it in this life; because if Thou dost not chastise me here in this life, I shall have to be chastised in the other world for all eternity. For this reason did St. Augustine say: "Lord, here cut, here burn, that you may spare during eternity." Chastise me here, O God, and do not spare me now, in order that I may be spared the punishment of hell. When the surgeon cuts the imposthume of the patient, it is a sign that he means to have him healed. St. Augustine says: "It is most merciful of the Lord not to suffer iniquity to pass unpunished."The Lord deals very mercifully with the sinner when by chastisement he makes him enter into himself in this life. Hence Job besought the Lord so earnestly to afflict him. And that this may be my comfort, that afflicting me with sorrow He spare not.

Jonas slept in the ship when he was flying from the Lord; but God seeing that the wretched man was on the brink of temporal and eternal death, caused him to be warned of the tempest: Why art thou fast asleep; rise up, call upon thy God. God, my brethren, now warns ye in like manner. You have been in the state of sin, deprived of sanctifying grace, the chastisement has come, and that chastisement is the voice of God, saying to you, "Why are you fast asleep, rise and call upon your God." Awake, sinner, do not live on forgetful of your soul and of God. Open your eyes, and see how you stand upon the verge of hell, where so many wretches are now bewailing sins less grievous than yours, and are you asleep, have you no thought of confession, no thought of rescuing yourself from eternal death? Rise, call upon your God. Up from that infernal pit into which you have fallen; pray to God to pardon you, beg of him this at least, if you are not at once resolved to change your life, that he will give you light, and make you see the wretched state in which you stand. Learn how to profit by the warning which the Lord vouch safes you. Jeremias first sees a rod. I see a rod watching; he next sees a boiling caldron: I see a boiling caldron. St. Ambrose, in speaking of this passage, explains it thus: He who is not corrected by the rod, shall be thrown into the caldron, there to burn. He whom the temporal chastisement fails to convert, shall be sent to burn eternally in hell-fire. Sinful brother, listen to God, who addresses himself to your heart, by this chastisement, and calls on you to do penance. Tell me what answer do you make him?

The prodigal son, after having left his father, thought no more upon him, whilst he continued to live amid delights; but when he saw himself reduced to that state of misery described in the Gospel, poor, deserted, obliged to tend swine, and not allowed to fill himself with the food wherewith the swine were filled, then he came to himself, and said: How many hired servants in my father's house abound with bread, and I here perish with hunger. I will arise and go to my father. And so he did, and was lovingly received by his father. Brother, you have to do in like manner. You see the unhappy life you have hitherto led, by living away from God; a life full of thorns and bitterness; a life which could not be otherwise, as being without God, who alone can give content. You see how many servants of God who love him lead a happy life, and enjoy continual peace, the peace of God, which, as the Apostle says, surpasses all the pleasures of the senses. The peace of God, which surpasseth all understanding. And what are you doing? Do you not feel that you suffer a hell in this life? Do you not know that you shall suffer one in the next? Take courage, say with the prodigal: I will arise and go to my father. I will arise from this sleep of death—this state of damnation, and return to God. It is true that I have sufficiently outraged him by leaving him so much against his desire, but he is still my Father. I will arise and go to my father. And when you shall go to that Father, what shall you say to him? Say what the prodigal said to his father: Father, I have sinned against heaven, and before thee; I am not now worthy to be called thy son. Father, I acknowledge my error, I have done ill to leave Thee, who have so much loved me; I see now that 1 am no longer worthy to be called Thy son; receive me at least as Thy servant; restore me at least to Thy grace, and then chastise me as Thou pleasest.

Oh, happy you, if you say and do thus, the same will happen you which befell the prodigal son. The father, when he saw his son retracing his steps, and perceived that he had humbled himself for his fault, not only did not drive him off—not only received him into his house, but embraced and kissed him as his son. And running to him, fell upon his neck and kissed him. He then clothed him with a precious garment, which represents the robe of grace: Bring forth quickly the first robe, and put it on him. And he, moreover, makes a great feast in the house, to commemorate the recovery of his son, whom he looked upon as lost and dead: Let us eat and make merry, because this my son was dead, and is come to life again; was lost, and is found.

Let us then be joyful, my brethren; it is true that God appears to be in wrath, but he is still our Father; let us retrace our steps in penance, and he will be appeased and spare us. Behold Mary our Mother praying for us on the one hand, and on the other turned towards us, saying, In me is all hope of life and of virtue; . . . come over to me all. My children, that Mother of Mercy says to us, My poor afflicted children, have recourse to me, and in me you shall find all hope; my Son denies me nothing. You were dead by sin; come to me, find me, and you shall find life—the life of divine grace, which I shall recover for you by my intercession. (Act of contrition.)

SEVENTH DISCOURSE.

God Chastises us in this Life, only that He may show us Mercy in the Next.

"Ego quos amo arguo et castigo."

"Such as I love, I rebuke and chastise."
—Apoc. 3:19.

WHEN the Lord had raised that great tempest which threatened to sink the ship in which Jonas was sailing, in punishment of his disobedience to the divine command, that he should preach to the Ninevites, everyone in the vessel was watching and in great fear, praying each to his God, with the exception of Jonas, who was asleep within the vessel: He fell into a deep sleep. But, knowing that he was the cause of the tempest, he caused himself to be thrown into the sea, and was there swallowed by the whale. When Jonas found himself in the body of that fish, and in such extreme danger of death, he addressed himself to God in prayer, and God delivered him: I cried out of my affliction to the Lord, and the Lord heard me. "Behold," says St. Zeno, "How Jonas, who slumbered in the ship, is awake in the whale." While in the ship, he slumbered in his sin; but when suffering chastisement, and upon the point of death, he opened his eyes and remembered God; hence he had recourse to the divine mercy which delivered him, causing the fish to leave him safe and sound upon the shore. Many persons, before seeing the divine chastisements, sleep in their sins, forgetful of God; but the Lord, because he does not desire their destruction, sends them afflictions, so that, roused from their lethargy, they return to him, and thus he is enabled to avoid punishing them during all eternity. The following is, then, the subject of this discourse: GOD PUNISHES US IN THIS LIFE, IN ORDER TO SPARE US IN THE NEXT.

We have not been created for this earth; we have been created for the blessed kingdom of Paradise. For this reason it is, says St. Augustine, that God mingles so much bitterness with the delights of the world in order that we may not forget him and eternal life. If, living as we do amid so many thorns in this life, we are strongly attached to it, and long so little after Paradise, how little should we not value Paradise if God were not to embitter continually the pleasures of this earth?

If we have offended God, we must needs be punished for it either in this world or in the next. St.

Ambrose says that God is merciful as well when he punishes as when he does not. The chastisements of God are the effect of his love; they are, to be sure, punishments, but punishments which ward off from us eternal punishment, and bring us to everlasting happiness. But whilst we are judged, we are chastised by the Lord, that we be not condemned with this world. And Judith reminded the Hebrews of the same truth when they were under the scourge of the Lord: Let us believe that these scourges of the Lord, with which like servants we are chastised, have happened for our amendment, and not for our destruction. Sara, the wife of Tobias, says the same: But of this every one is sure that worshippeth Thee: . . . if his life be under correction, it shall be allowed to come to Thy mercy, for Thou art not delighted in our being lost. Lord, she said, Thou chastisest us here in order that Thou mayest spare us in the other life, for Thou dost not desire our destruction.

We have it from God himself that those whom he loves in this life he chastises in order that they may be converted: Those whom I love I rebuke and chastise. Where God loves, says St. Basil of Seleucia, severity is usually the pledge of his graces. Unhappy are the sinners who living in the state of sin prosper in this life; it is a sign that (rod reserves them for everlasting punishment. The sinner hath provoked the Lord; according to the multitude of His wrath, He will not seek him. Behold, says St. Augustine, speaking of the passage quoted, behold the most grievous chastisement! When he does not appear to take notice of the sinner, and leaves him unpunished, it is a sign that he is very wroth. I call you, says God to him whom he chastises, and will you be deaf to my voice? Son, be converted, otherwise you shall confirm my anger, since I shall cease to regard your salvation, and allow you to live on in your sins without punishment, but only that I may punish you in the life to come. And My indignation shall rest in thee; and My jealousy shall depart from thee, and I will cease and be angry no more. The Apostle warns you, my brethren, not to be deaf to the voice of God, for that on the Day of Judgment your obstinacy shall be rewarded with a dreadful chastisement, and that chastisement eternal. But according to thy hardness and impenitent heart thou treasurest up to thyself wrath against the day of wrath, and revelation of the just judgment of God, who will render to every man according to his works.

So that, St. Jerome says, that there cannot be a

greater punishment for a sinner than that he should not be punished in this life. And St. Isidore of Pelusium says that sinners who are punished in this life do not deserve pity, but those only who die without having been punished. It is not so bad, continues the saint, to be simply sick as to have no one to cure you. St. Augustine says, in another part, that when God does not chastise the sinner in this world, he chastises him most severely; whence he concludes that there is no greater misfortune than impunity for a sinner. After England had rebelled against the Church, God did not visit her with temporal scourges: her riches have been increasing from that time; but her chastisement is all the greater on that account, as she is left to perish in her sin. The absence of punishment is the greatest punishment, says the same holy Doctor. The not receiving chastisement in this life for sin is a great chastisement, and prosperity in sin a still greater.

Why then, Job inquires, do the wicked live, are they advanced and strengthened with richest? How comes it, O Lord, that sinners, instead of being taken out of this life in poverty and tribulation, enjoy health, and honors, and riches? The holy man answers, They spend their days in wealth, and in a moment they go down to hell. Wretched men, they enjoy their riches for a few days, and when the hour of chastisement comes, when they least expect it, they are condemned to burn forever in that place of torments. Jeremiah makes the self-same inquiry: Why doth the way of the wicked prosper? And then adds, Gather them together as sheep for a sacrifice. Animals destined for sacrifice are kept from all labor, and fattened up for slaughter. Thus does God act towards the obstinate: he abandons them, and suffers them to fatten on the pleasures of this life in order to sacrifice them in the other to his eternal justice; for these, says Minutius Felix, are fed like victims for the slaughter.

These wretched men, says David, shall not be punished in this life, they shall enjoy their fleeting pleasures; by and by their dream shall have ceased: Neither shall they be scourged like other men; . . . they have suddenly ceased to be; as the dream of them that awake, O Lord, so in Thy city Thou shalt bring their image to nothing. How painful is not the case of a poor man, who dreams that he has grown rich or great, and upon awaking finds himself the miserable and sick creature he is? And the enemies of the Lord shall . . . vanish like smoke. The happiness of sinners is as suddenly dissipated as is smoke by a breath of air. "Smoke," observes St. Gregory, in his comment upon this passage, "Vanishes in its ascent." And the same is the case with sinners: I have seen the wicked highly exalted, . . . and I passed by, and lo, he was not. Minutius Felix says, in his comment upon the place cited, the unhappy men are exalted the higher, that their fall may be the greater. The Lord allows the sinner to be exalted for his greater punishment, in order that his fall may be the more grievous, as is said by David. When they were lifted up Thou hast cast them down. If the sick man, says St. John Chrysostom, suffer hunger or thirst by order of his physician, it is a sign that the physician has hopes of him; but if the doctor allow him to eat what he pleases, and drink as much as he likes, what are we to conclude from that? It is plain that the physician has given him over. And thus, says St. Gregory, it is a manifest sign that God abandons the sinner to perdition, when he never thwarts his evil purposes: and in the Book of Proverbs we read that the prosperity of fools shall destroy them. As lightning precedes thunder, says St. Bernard, so is prosperity the forerunner of damnation for the sinner.

The greatest punishment inflicted by God is, when he allows the sinner to sleep on in sin, without rousing him from that sleep of death in which he is buried. I will make them drunk, that they may sleep an everlasting sleep, and awake no more, saith the Lord. Cain, after the crime of murdering his brother, was afraid that he should be killed by the first person he should meet: Everyone therefore that findeth me shall kill me. But the Lord assured him that he should live, and that no one should kill him; which assurance of a long life, according to St. Ambrose, was Cain's greatest punishment. The saint says, that God treats the obstinate sinner mercifully, when he gives him an early death, because he thus saves him from as many hells as he should have committed sins during a longer life. Let sinners, then, live according to the desires of their hearts, let them enjoy their pleasures in peace; there will at length come a time when they shall be caught as fish upon the hook. As fishes are taken with the hook, . . . so men are taken in the evil time. Whence St. Augustine says, "Do not rejoice like the fish who is delighted with the bait, for the fisherman has not yet pulled the hook." If you were to see a condemned man making merry at a banquet with the halter round his neck, and every moment awaiting the order for execution, would you envy or pity him? Neither should you envy the sinner who is happy in his vices. That wretched sinner is already on the hook, he is already in the infernal net; when the time of chastisement shall have arrived, then the wretch will know and deplore his damnation, but all to no purpose.

On the contrary, it is a good sign when a sinner is chastised and suffers tribulation in this life: it is a sign that God has still merciful views upon him, and that he wishes to substitute a temporal for an eternal punishment in his regard. God, says St. John Chrysostom, when he punishes us on this earth, does not do so out of hatred to us, but that he may draw us to himself. He chastises for a little while, that he may have you with him for eternity. When the physician uses the knife, he does so to cure, says St. Augustine. And God, the saint continues, does the same in our regard. "God seems to be cruel; but do not fear; for he is a father who is never cruel, and does not wish to destroy us." But, does not God say the same himself? Those, whom I love, I rebuke and chastise; be zealous therefore, and do penance. Son, says God, I love you, and therefore I chastise you; "Be zealous;" see how good I am to you; endeavor you to act in like manner towards me; do penance for your sins, if you wish that I should spare you the chastisement which you deserve: at least, accept with patience and turn to advantage the tribulation which I send you. In this cross which now afflicts you hear you my voice calling upon you to turn to me, and fly from hell, which is close upon you. Behold! I stand at the gate and knock; lam knocking at the door of your heart; open then to me, and know that when the sinner who has driven me from his heart shall open the door again to me, I will enter, and keep him company forever. If any man shall hear My voice, and open to Me the door, Twill come in to him, and will sup with him, and he with Me. I shall remain united to him forever on this earth; and if he remain faithful, I shall seat him beside me, on the throne of my eternal kingdom. To him that shall overcome, I will give to sit with Me in My throne.

What, must we look upon God as a tyrant, who should take pleasure in our sufferings? He does take pleasure in punishing us, but exactly the same pleasure as a father takes in correcting his son: he does not take pleasure in the pain which he inflicts, but in the amendment it will work. My son, reject not the correction of the Lord; and do not faint when thou art chastised by Him, for whom the Lord loveth He chastiseth, and as a father in the son, He pleaseth Himself. He chastises you because he loves you; it is not that he wishes to see you afflicted, but converted; and if he takes pleasure in your suffering, he does so inasmuch as it is an instrument of conversion—just as a father who chastises his son derives pleasure, not from the affliction of his son, but from the amendment which he hopes to see in him, and which will prevent him from working his own ruin. Chastisement makes us return to God, says St. John Chrysostom; and it is to this end God inflicts it, in order that we may not stay away from him.

Why then, my brethren, do you complain of God when in tribulation? You ought to thank him prostrate on the earth; tell me now, if a man condemned to die were to have his sentence changed by the prince from death into one hour's imprisonment, and if he were to complain of that one hour, would his complaint be justifiable? Oh, would he not rather deserve that the prince should reverse the last sentence, and condemn him a second time to death? You have long and often deserved hell by your sins. And do you know all that the word hell conveys? Know that it is more dreadful to suffer for one moment in hell than to suffer for a hundred years the most frightful torments which the martyrs have suffered on earth; and in this hell you should have had to suffer during all eternity. And yet you complain if God send you some tribulation, some infirmity, some loss. Thank God, and say: Lord, this chastisement is trifling compared with my sins. I ought to have been in hell burning, deserted by all, and in despair: I thank you for having called me to yourself by this tribulation which you have sent me. God, says Oleaster, often calls sinners to repentance by temporal chastisements. By earthly chastisements the Lord shows us the immense punishment which our sins deserve; and therefore afflicts us on this earth, that we may be converted and escape eternal flames.

Wretched, then, as we have been, wretched indeed is that sinner who is left unpunished in this life, but still more wretched he who, admonished by affliction, does not amend, says St. Basil. It is not a grievous thing to be afflicted by God on this earth after one has sinned; but it is very grievous not to be converted by the affliction sent, and to be like those of whom David speaks, who, although visited by the divine chastisement, still sleep on in their sins. At Thy rebuke, O God of Jacob, they have all slumbered. As if the sound of the scourges and the thunders of God, instead of rousing them from their lethargy, served only to make them sleep more soundly. I struck you, yet you returned not to Me. I have scourged you, says God, in order that you might return to me; but ye, ungrateful that you are, have been deaf to my calls. Unhappy the sinner who acts like him of whom the Lord says, He shall send lightnings against him; . . . his heart shall be as hard as a stone, and as firm as a smith's anvil. God visits him with chastisement, and he, instead of being softened and returning to the Lord by penance, shall be as firm as a smiths anvil; he shall grow more hardened under the blows of God, as the anvil grows continually harder under the hammer of the smith; and shall become like the impious Achaz, of whom the scripture says, In the time of his distress he increased contempt against the Lord. Unhappy man, instead of humbling himself, he the more despised the Lord.

Do you know what more happens to these rash beings? They begin to suffer hell even in this life. He shall rain snares upon the sinners; fire and brimstone and storms of wind shall be the portion of their cup. The Lord shall rain upon them his chastisement, sickness, misery, and every bitterness; but this is not the entire, it is only a portion of their cup, that is, of their chastisement. "The Lord says, the portion only of their cup," observes St. Gregory; "Because their suffering begins here indeed, but shall be continued throughout eternity." He deserves all this who, being afflicted by the Lord for his conversion, continues to earn chastisement, and provoke the Lord to greater wrath, says St. Augustine. What can I do, O sinner, to work your conversion, will the Lord then say. I have called you by sermons and inspirations, and you have despised them; I have called you by favors, and you have grown more insolent; I have called you by scourges, and you continue to offend me. For what shall I strike you anymore, you that increase transgression; . . . and the daughter of Sion shall be left as a city that is laid waste. Do you not wish to hearken even to my chastisements? Do you wish that I should abandon you? I shall be obliged to do it if you do not amend.

My brethren, let us no longer abuse the mercy which God uses towards us. Let us not be like the nettle, which stings him who strikes it. God afflicts us, because he loves us, and wishes to see us reformed, says Oleaster. When we feel the chastisement, we should bethink us of our sins, and say with the brethren of Joseph, We de serve to suffer these things, because we have sinned against our brother. Lord, Thou punishest us justly, because we have offended Thee, our Father and God. Thou art just, O God, and Thy judgment is right. Everything Thou hast done to us, Thou hast done in true judgment. Lord, Thou art just, and dost with justice punish us; we accept this tribulation which Thou sendest us; give us strength to suffer it with patience.

Here we should do well to remember what God once said to a nun: "You have sinned, you must do penance, you must pray." Some sinners are satisfied with recommending themselves to the servants of God, but they must moreover pray and do penance. Let us do so, because when the Lord shall see our resignation he will not only forgive our sins, but even remit the chastisement; and if God continues to afflict us, let us have recourse to that Lady, who is called the consolatrix of the afflicted. All the saints compassionate us in our sufferings, but there is not of them, as St. Antoninus says, who feels so much for us as this divine Mother Mary. And Richard of St. Victor adds, that this Mother of mercy cannot behold unhappy sufferers without succoring them. (Act of contrition.)

EIGHTH DISCOURSE.

Prayers Appease God, and Avert from us the Chastisement we Deserve, provided we purpose to Amend.

"Petite et accipietis, quærite et invenietis."

"Ask and you shall receive, seek and you shall find." —John, 16:24.

HE who has a good heart cannot but feel compassion for the afflicted, and wish to see all men happy. But who has a heart as good as the Lord's? He by his nature is infinite goodness, whence it is that God by his nature has an extreme desire to deliver us from every evil, and render us happy in all things, nay, even partakers of his own happiness. He wishes, therefore, that for our greater good we beg of him the graces which we stand in need of, that we may be spared the chastisement which we deserve, and arrive at life everlasting. Hence he has promised to hear the prayers of him who prays to him with hope in his goodness. Ask and you shall receive.

But to come at once to the subject of our discourse: GOD IS APPEASED BY PRAYERS, AND LED TO WITHDRAW THE CHASTISEMENT WHICH WE DESERVE, PROVIDED WE PURPOSE TO AMEND.

Hence in order to be delivered from the present scourge, and still more from the eternal scourge, WE MUST PRAY AND HOPE. This is to be the first point.—But it is not sufficient to pray and to hope: WE MUST PRAY AND HOPE AS WE OUGHT. This is to be the second point.

1. WE MUST AND HOPE.

God wishes that we should all be saved, as the Apostle assures us: God, Who will have all men to be saved. And although he sees so many sinners who deserve hell, he does not wish that any of them should be lost, but that they should be restored to his grace by penance, and be saved. Not willing that any should perish, but that all should return to penance. But before delivering us from the punishment we have deserved, and dispensing his graces, he wishes to be sought in prayer. "By prayer," says St. Laurence Justinian, "The wrath of God is suspended, his vengeance is delayed, and pardon finally procured." Oh how great are the promises which God makes to him who prays! Call upon Me in the day of trouble, and I will deliver thee. Cry to Me, and I will hear thee. You shall ask whatever you will, and it shall be done unto you. Theodoret says that prayer is one only instrument, but that it can effect all things. And let us bear in mind, my brethren, that when we pray and ask things conducive to salvation, not even our sins can prevent our receiving the graces which we beg.—For every one that asketh receiveth. Jesus Christ here says that whoever asks, be he just or in sin, shall receive. Wherefore did David say, For Thou, O Lord, art sweet and mild, and plenteous in mercy to all that call upon Thee. Hence the Apostle St. James, in order to excite us to prayer, tells us: But if any of you want wisdom, let him ask of God, who giveth to all men abundantly, and upbraideth not. When God is solicited, he gives more than is asked of him, he giveth to all men abundantly. When one man asks a favor of another whom he may have formerly injured, the latter usually reproaches him with the injury that had been done him; but not so God—he never upbraideth. When we beg of him some grace for the good of our souls, he never reproaches us with the offences which we have committed against him; but he hears us, and consoles us as though we had always served him faithfully. Hitherto you have not asked anything in My name, said the Lord one day to his disciples, and today he says the same thing to us: Ask, and you shall receive, that your joy may be full. As if he were to say, Why do you complain of me? You have only yourselves to blame—you have not asked graces of me, and therefore you have not received them. Ask of me, henceforward, what you please, and it shall be granted you; and if you have not merit sufficient to obtain it, ask it of my Father in my name, that is, through my merits, and whatever it be, I promise you that you shall obtain it. Amen, amen, I say to you; if you ask the Father anything in My name, He will give it to you. The princes of the earth, says St. John Chrysostom, give audience only to a few, and that seldom; but access can always be had to God by everyone, at all times, and with certainty of a favorable hearing.

Rely, then, upon these great promises, so often repeated by the Lord in the Scriptures; and let us ever be attentive to beg of him those graces which are necessary for salvation, namely, the pardon of our sins, perseverance in his grace, his holy love, resignation to his divine will, a happy death, and Paradise. By prayer we shall attain all; without prayer we shall have nothing. What the holy Fathers and theologians commonly say, namely, that prayer is necessary to adults, as a means of salvation, comes to this, that it is impossible for anyone to be saved without prayer. Lessius wisely says, that it ought to be of faith; that without prayer salvation is impossible to adults. And this is clearly to be drawn from the Scriptures, which say: Ask, and you shall receive: for as he who seeks obtains, says St. Theresa, he who does not seek does not obtain. Pray that ye enter not into temptation. We ought always to pray. The words "Seek," and "Pray," and "We ought," according to the opinions of most theologians, along with St. Thomas, imply a precept binding under pain of mortal sin.

Let us pray, then, and pray with great confidence. Confidence in what? In that divine promise by which, says St. Augustine, God has made himself our debtor. He has promised; he cannot be wanting to his promise; let us seek and hope, and we must be saved. No one hath hoped in the Lord, and hath been confounded. There never has been and never will be found any one to hope in the Lord and be lost, as the prophet assures us: He is the protector of all that trust in Him.

But how comes it, then, that some persons ask graces and do not obtain them? St. James answers that it is because they ask ill. You ask, and receive not, because you ask amiss. You must not only ask and hope, but ask and hope as you ought. This brings us to the second point.

2. WE MUST HOPE AND PRAY AS WE OUGHT.

God has all the desire to deliver us from every evil, and to share his blessings with us, as I said in the beginning, but he wishes to be sought in prayer, and prayed to as he should, in order that we should be heard. How can God think of hearing that sinner who prays to him that he may be freed from his afflictions, whilst he is unwilling to abandon sin, which is the cause of his afflictions? When the impious Jeroboam stretched out his hand against the prophet, who reproached him with his wretchedness, the Lord caused his hand to wither up, so that he could not draw it back. *And his hand which he stretched forth against him withered, and he was not able to draw it back again to him.* Then the king turned to the man of God, and besought him to beg of the Lord to restore his hand to him. Theodoret says, with regard to this circumstance:

"Fool that he was to have asked the prophet's prayers for the restoration of his hand, and not for pardon of his sins." Thus do many act; they beg of God to deliver them from their afflictions; they beg of the servants of God to avert by their prayers the threatened chastisements, but they do not seek to obtain the grace of abandoning their sins and changing their lives. And how can such persons hope to be freed from the chastisement when they will not remove its cause? What arms the hand of the Lord with thunders to chastise and afflict us? Oh, it is accursed sin! "Punishment is the fine that is to be paid for sin," says Tertullian. The afflictions we suffer are a fine which must be paid by him whom sin has subjected to the penalty. St. Basil in like manner says that sin is a note of hand which we give against ourselves. Since we sin, we voluntarily go in debt to God's justice. It is not God, then, who makes us miserable; it is sin. Sin it is which obliges God to create chastisements: Famine, and affliction, and scourges, all things are created for the wicked.

Jeremias, addressing the divine vengeance, says, O thou sword of the Lord, how long wilt thou not be quiet? Go into thy scabbard, rest and be still. But then, he goes on to say, How shall it be quiet when the Lord hath given it a charge against Ascalon? How can the sword of the Lord ever be quiet if sinners do not choose to abandon their sin, notwithstanding that the Lord has given a charge to his sword to execute vengeance as long as sinners shall continue to deserve it? But some will say, we make novenas, we fast, we give alms, we pray to God: why are we not heard? To them the Lord replies, When they fast, I will not hear their prayers, and when they offer holocausts and victims, I will not receive them; for I will consume them by the sword, and by famine, and by pestilence. How, exclaims the Lord, how can I hear the prayers of those who beg to be freed from their afflictions, and not from their sins, because they do not wish to reform. What care I for their fasts, and their sacrifices, and their alms, when they will not change their lives. I will consume them by the sword. With all their prayers, and devotions, and penitential exercises, I shall be obliged by my justice to punish them.

Let us not, then, my brethren, trust to prayers or other devotions, unaccompanied by a resolution to amend. You pray, you smite your breast, and call for mercy; but that is not enough. The impious Antiochus prayed, but the Scriptures say that his prayers failed to obtain mercy from God. Then this wicked man prayed to the Lord, of whom he was not to obtain mercy. The unhappy man, finding himself devoured by worms, and near his end, prayed for life, but without having sorrow for his sins.

Nor let us trust in our holy protectors, if we do not purpose to amend. Some say we have our patron or some other saint who will defend us; we have our Mother Mary to procure our deliverance. Bring forth therefore fruit worthy of penance. Who hath showed you to flee from the wrath to come? . . . and think not to say within yourselves, we have Abraham for our father. How can we think to escape punishment if we do not abandon sin? How can the saints think of assisting us if we persist in exasperating the Lord? St. John Chrysostom says, of what use was Jeremias to the Jews? The Jews had Jeremias to pray for them, but, notwithstanding all the prayers of that holy prophet, they received the chastisement, because they did not wish to give up their sins. Beyond doubt, says the holy Doctor, the prayers of the saints contribute much to obtain the divine mercy for us, but when?— when we do penance. They are useful, but only when we do ourselves violence to abandon sin, to fly occasions, and return to God's favor.

The emperor Phocas, in order to defend himself from his enemies, raised walls and multiplied fortifications, but he heard a voice saying to him from heaven: "You build walls, but when the enemy is within, the city is easily taken." We must then expel this enemy, which is sin, from our souls, otherwise God cannot exempt us from chastisement, because he is just, and cannot leave sin unpunished. Another time the citizens of Antioch prayed to Mary to avert from them a scourge which overhung them; and whilst they were praying, St. Bertoldus heard the divine Mother replying from heaven, "Abandon your sins, and I shall be propitious to you."

Let us then beg of the Lord to use mercy towards us, but let us pray as David prayed: Lord, incline unto my aid. God wishes to aid us, but he wishes that we should aid ourselves, by doing all that depends upon us. "He who desires to be assisted," says Hilaretus, "Must do all that he can to assist himself." God wishes to save us, but we must not imagine that God will do all without our doing anything. St. Augustine says: "He who created you without your help will not save you without your help." What do you expect, sinful brother? That

God will bring you to Paradise with all your sins upon you? Do you continue to draw down upon you the divine scourges, and yet hope to be delivered from them? Must God save you while you persist in damning yourself?

If we purpose truly to turn to God, then let us pray to him and rejoice; even though the sins of the entire world were ours, we should be heard, as I said to you in the beginning. Everyone who prays with a purpose of amendment, obtains mercy. Let our prayers be in the name of Jesus Christ, who has promised that the eternal Father will grant us everything we ask in his name, that is, through his merits. If you ask the Father anything in My name, He will give it to you. Let us pray, and never cease from prayer; thus we shall obtain every grace, and save ourselves. It is to this we are exhorted by St. Bernard, who tells us to pray to God through the intercession of Mary: "Let us seek grace, and seek it through Mary; because he who seeks through her, obtains his request, and cannot be disappointed." Mary, when we pray to her, certainly pleads for us with her Son; and when Mary prays for us, she obtains what she demands, and her prayer cannot be refused by a son who loves her so much. (Act of contrition.)

NINTH DISCOURSE.

Most Holy Mary is the Mediatrix of Sinners.

"Ego murus et ubera mea sicut turris; ex quo factus sum coram eo quasi pacem reperiens."

"I am a wall, and my breasts are as a tower, since I am become in his presence as one finding peace."—Cant. 8:10.

DIVINE grace is an infinite treasure, because it makes us friends of God. For she is an infinite treasure to men, which they that use become the friends of God. Hence it follows, that if there cannot be a greater happiness than to enjoy the grace of God, there cannot be a greater misery than to incur his displeasure by sin, which makes us his enemies. But to God the wicked and his wickedness are hateful alike. But if, my brethren, any of you have had the misfortune to forfeit this divine grace by sin, do not despair, but console yourselves with the reflection, that you have in Jesus Christ himself a mediator, who can obtain pardon for you, and restore you the grace you have lost. And He is the propitiation for our sins.

What have you to fear, says St. Bernard, when you can have recourse to so great a mediator? He can do all things with his eternal Father. He has satisfied the divine justice for you, continues the holy abbot, and has nailed your sins to the cross, having taken them away from your soul. But if, notwithstanding all this, you fear to approach Jesus Christ on account of his divine majesty, God has given you another advocate with his Son, and that advocate is Mary.

Thus Mary has been given to the world as a mediatrix between God and sinners. Hear the words which the Holy Ghost makes her speak in the divine canticles: I am a wall, and my breasts are as a tower, since I am become in His presence as one finding peace. I am, she says, the refuge of those who fly to me; my breasts, that is, my mercy, are like a tower of defence to everyone who has recourse to me; and he who is the enemy of God, let him know that I am the mediatrix of peace between God and sinners. "She finds peace for enemies, salvation for the lost, mercy for those who are in despair," says Cardinal Hugo. For this reason is Mary called beautiful . . . as the curtains of Solomon? In the tents of David naught was to be heard of but war; in the tents of Solomon naught is spoken of but peace. By this we are to understand that Mary has no other ministry in heaven than that of peace and pardon. Hence St. Andrew Avellino calls her the pleader of Paradise; but what are those occupations in which Mary is engaged? "Mary," says Venerable Bede, "Stands in the presence of her Son, praying unceasingly for sinners."And Blessed Amadeus says that "Mary, all-powerful by her prayers, stands before the face of God, continually interceding for us." Thus Mary never ceases to implore of God by her all-powerful prayers all graces for us, if we do not refuse them. And are there any found to re fuse the graces solicited for them by this divine Mother? Yes, there are found such—yes, those who will not abandon sin, who will not give up this friendship, this occasion; who will not restore their neighbor's property—those are they who will not receive the graces begged for them by Mary, because Mary wishes to obtain for them the grace of breaking off this connection; of flying this occasion of weakness, and they will not do it. And such as will not do it, positively refuse the grace sought for them by Mary. From heaven she sees well all our miseries and dangers; and oh, how deeply is she touched with compassion for us! With what motherly affection is she always endeavoring to assist us! "For she sees our dangers," continues the Blessed Amadeus, "And as our merciful Sovereign compassionates us with maternal affection."

One day St. Bridget heard Jesus Christ saying to Mary: "Mother, ask of me what you will." And Mary answered him: "I ask mercy for the unfortunate." As if she were to say to him, Son, since Thou hast made me the Mother of mercy, and Advocate of Sinners, can I ask aught else of Thee than mercy for the unhappy? In a word, St. Augustine says, that amongst all the saints, we have not one who is so solicitous for our salvation as Mary.

Isaias complains in his day as follows: Behold, Thou art angry; . . . there is none who riseth up and taketh hold of Thee. Lord, said the prophet, Thou art justly angry with us for our sins, and there is no one to appease Thee, or draw Thee from chastising us. St. Bonaventure says that the prophet had reason .to speak thus, since there was no Mary then. But at present, if Jesus Christ wishes to chastise a sinner, and the sinner recommends himself to Mary, she by her prayers for him restrains her Son, and averts the chastisement from him. There is no one, he says, so well able to hold back the sword of the Lord. Justly, then, did St. Andrew call Mary the peace of the Lord with men. And St. Justin called her the "Arbitress," saying, "The Word uses the Virgin as arbitress." Sequestra signifies an arbitress, to whose decision disputants bind themselves to yield. By which St. Justin means to say, that Jesus lays before Mary all his reasons for punishing such a sinner, that she may negotiate a peace; and the sinner, on the other side, places himself in her hands. Thus Mary on the one side obtains for the sinner the grace of amendment, and penance on the other; she obtains pardon for him of her Son, and thus it is concluded. Such is the ministry in the exercise of which Mary is continually occupied.

When Noe judged that the deluge ought to have ceased, he dismissed the dove from the ark. It returned with a branch of olive, significant of the peace which God had concluded with the world. This dove was a figure of Mary. "Thou art," says St. Bonaventure, "That most faithful dove of Noe which became the most faithful mediatrix between God and the world submerged by a spiritual deluge." Thou, O Mary, art the dove all faithful to him who invokes Thee—Thou art the dove that, interceding with God, hast obtained for us peace and salvation, says St. Epiphanius. Pelbart inquires how it happens that in the .Old Law, the Lord was so vigorous in his chastisements, of universal deluge, of fire from heaven, of fiery serpents, and such like punishments; whereas he now deals so mercifully with us, who have sinned more grievously than those of old? And he answers, he does it all through love of Mary, who intercedes for us. "Oh how long since should heaven and earth have been destroyed," says St. Fulgentius, "If Mary had not interposed."

Wherefore the Church wishes that we should call this divine Mother our hope. The impious Luther could not endure that the Church should teach us to call Mary our hope. He said that our hope ought to rest only in God—not in the creature; and that God curses him who places his confidence in creatures: Cursed be the man that trusteth in man. True; but that is understood of those who trust in creatures, in contempt of God, or independently of him. But we hope in Mary, as our mediatrix with the Lord. In the same manner as Jesus is our mediator of right with his eternal Father, because by the merits of his Passion he obtains pardon for penitent sinners, so Mary is mediatrix by divine favor with her Son, and is such a mediatrix that her Son grants her every request; nay, that he wishes that every grace should pass through her hands. "The Lord," says St. Bernard, "Has placed in Mary the plenitude of all good; so that if aught of hope or grace or salvation, is in us, we know that we derive it from Mary." The Lord has confided to Mary the treasure of mercies which he wishes to have dealt out to us, and therefore wishes that we should acknowledge every grace as coming through her. Whence the saint calls her his chief confidence, and the principal ground of his hope. For which reason he exhorts us to look for grace always through the intercession of Mary. And for the same reason the Church, in despite of Luther, calls Mary our hope.

Hence also do the saints call Mary the ladder, the moon, and the city of refuge. She is called by St. Bernard the ladder of sinners. It is sin which separates us from God. But your iniquities have divided between you and your God. A soul in the state of grace is in union with God, and God in union with it. He that abideth in charity, abideth in God, and God in him. But when the soul turns its back upon God, then is it separated from him—plunged into an abyss of misery, and as far removed from him as sin itself. But when shall this wretched soul find a ladder by which to mount once more to

God, and be again united to him? Mary is that ladder, to whom, if the sinner has recourse, no matter what his misery, or how great the filth of sins, he can come out of the pit of perdition. "Thou," says St. Bernard, "Dost not abhor the sinner, however loathsome he be; if he once sigh to thee, thou readiest him thy hand to draw him out of the gulf of despair." For the same reason is she called the moon: Fair as the moon. "As the moon," says St. Bernard, "Is placed between the sun and earth, so is Mary stationed between God and us, to pour out his graces continually upon us." Hence, also, she is called the city of refuge, as she is made to call herself by St. John Damascene. "I am the city of all those that have recourse to me." In the ancient law there were five cities of sanctuary; to which, if anyone fled, he was secure of not being pursued by justice, no matter what his crime. At present we have not so many cities of sanctuary—we have only Mary, to whom if any one shall have fled he may rest secure of not being pursued by the divine justice. In the cities of the old law every delinquent was in danger, nor could all his crimes escape unpunished; but Mary is a city of refuge which receives every criminal. "There is no one so much cast off by God," said this blessed Mother to St. Bridget, "Who, if he have recourse to me, shall not return to God, and receive pardon."

Mary, so far from disdaining to assist sinners, prides herself upon the function of advocate of sinners, so that she is related to have said to the venerable sister Mary Villanin, "Next to my dignity of Mother of God, there is nothing which I so much value as my office of advocate of sinners." "To this end," says Idiota, who takes it from St. John Chrysostom, "Hast thou been chosen from eternity to be the Mother of God, that those whose sins should exclude them from participation in the merits of thy Son might be made partakers of them by thy intercession." This was the principal office for the fulfillment of which God created her, and placed her in the world: Feed thy kids. By kids he means sinners, and those kids are given in care to Mary, in order that they who on the day of judgment should by their sins have deserved to stand upon the left, may by her intercession stand upon the right. "Feed thy kids," says William of Paris, "Whom thou shalt convert into sheep, that they who should have been placed to the left may through thy intercession take their stand upon the right." But we must not forget to notice what has been said upon this passage by William of England: "Feed thy kids." Who are the kids of Mary?

"These sinners," he says, "Who pay her no devotion, who do not beg of her to obtain their conversion, are not the kids of Mary, and shall be placed on the left."

St. Bridget one day heard Jesus Christ saying to his mother, "Thou givest assistance to everyone endeavoring to rise to God." Mary assists everyone who does himself violence to leave his evil life and turn to God, or at least prays to her that he may receive strength to do so; if he have not that desire, the divine mother herself cannot assist him. Mary then assists only those sinners who honor her by some special devotion, and who, if they yet remain in disgrace with God, have recourse to her that she may obtain pardon for them, and work their deliverance from their present infernal condition. The sinner who acts thus from his heart is secure, because Mary, as we have said before, has been therefore created that she might have charge of sinners, and lead them to God. The Lord revealed this to St.
Catherine of Sienna: "She is chosen by me as a most delicious food, so as to capture men, especially sinners." And the blessed Mother herself said to St. Bridget, that as the magnet attracts iron, so she draws the hard hearts of men to herself and

to God. But we must always bear in mind that these hearts, notwithstanding their hardness, must desire liberation from their unhappy state.

Ah, if all had recourse to Mary with at least this desire, she would procure salvation for all. "What fear of damnation should that man feel," says the Abbot Adam, "To whom Mary offers herself for a mother and an advocate?" He inquires again, "Could it be possible that you, the mother of mercy, should not intercede with the Redeemer for the soul he has redeemed?" He lastly makes answer: "Ah, Thou must intercede, because God, who has placed his Son mediator between man and heaven, has placed Thee mediatrix between his Son and guilty man."

Then, sinner, says St. Bernard, give thanks to him who has provided you with such a mediatrix. Thank your God, who, in order to manifest his mercy towards you, has given you not only his Son for a mediator in his own right, but that you might have more confidence, has given you Mary as a mediatrix with that Son. Therefore it is St. Augustine calls her the only hope of sinners. And St. Bonaventure: "If by reason of your iniquities you see the Lord in anger, and fear to approach him, have recourse to the hope of sinners, who is Mary." She will not reject you because you are too wretched; "It is her office to assist the wretched." And William of Paris says exactly the same: "It is thy office to place thyself between God and man." Hence, when we have recourse to Mary, let everyone say to her with St. Thomas of Villanova: "Ah, therefore, thou our advocate fulfill thy office." Since thou art Mother of God, and advocate of the wretched, assist me who am so wretched; if thou dost not assist me, I am lost; and let us proceed to address her in the words of St. Bernard: "Remember, O most pious virgin, that from the beginning, etc., etc." I do not wish to be the first unhappy man who shall have had recourse to thee, and yet be abandoned by thee. (Act of contrition.)